To Mark &
Thank you for sha
home with us :)
Mike Caroline

WEC INTERNATIONAL

Leaves to the Nations

Stories from Canadian WEC missionaries

First published by WEC International 2025

This book was written to celebrate 100 years of WEC International (Worldwide Evangelization for Christ) activity in Canada. The stories were written by many WECers (as we call them) over many years working in many countries; they were compiled and edited by Marian den Boer.

Cover design by Dania & Leyla Varela (Canadian MKs)

First edition

ISBN: 978-0-9681685-1-6

This book was professionally typeset on Reedsy.
Find out more at reedsy.com

Contents

Note from the Editor	ix
Preface	x
WEC International in Canada - History	xii

I Seeds

Sharing with a Busload of People	3
A Prayer Walk	5
The Valley and the Ditches	6
Following that Still Small Voice	8
Only a Mustard Seed of Confidence	10
Only the Holy Spirit Knows	11
Planting Seeds at an Eid Kabir Celebration	12
Small Seeds	14
Worshipping in the Marketplace	18

II Divine Encouragement

Jesus Speaks	23
Two Streetcar Tickets	24
Powerful Pray-ers	26
Life Comes from Above	28

III Answering the Call

Called to Africa 33
The Story of our Calling 37
God Affirms Jason's Call 42
How I got into Missions 44
Walk With Me 46
Remembering My Husband - Pilot Don Collins 49
Melissa Meets Jesus 51
Even during War God Makes a Way 54
I Surrender All 56

IV Missionary Life

A Year of Mishaps and Miracles 59
Pioneering Medical Work 63
Establishing a School is a Priority 65
Pioneering 67
Feeling Like an Outcast 75
The Opienge Revival 77
God's Grace, Love and Power Demonstrated 78
Handling a Missionary Medical Career and Motherhood 81
Missionary Boy 86
Divine Protection 87
Picnicking in the Hills 88
50 And Rising 89
Re-book your Tickets! 92
They were Looking for Guns 98
Basking in His Presence 100
A Little Child Shall Lead Them 101
A Close Call 102

V Despite Persecution

Hallelujah Street 107
Psalm 16 110
Saved from the Fire 117
Torrential Baptism 119
The Troublesome Tract 122

VI Evangelizing

A Birthday Party 129
A Spiritual Battle 131
When God Opens the Heart 134
She said, "I Believe" 138
Opportunity Knocks 140
Saved through Revelation 142
The Nanny 146
Treasure in the Garbage Can 148
When Jesus Opens the Door 151

VII Discipling

Breaking Bondages 155
Alejandro's Story 159
Joseph finds the Truth 161
More Than a Chance Encounter 163

VIII First Things First

Co-Workers 169
First Barala Convert 171
First Women's Conference 173
First, We Learn the Alphabet 177

Ready Or Not, Here I Come 179
While Buying a Table 180

IX Following His Promptings

A Word in Season 183
Following the God of the Impossible 185
Cheating Death 187
Confronting a Wife-beater 189
The Reluctant Leader 191
Wisdom from God 193

X As Led by the Holy Spirit

A Dream about a Dove 197
The Lighthouse on Market Street 198
Bible Study in a Muslim Home 202
Countering The Communists 204
In Search of a Green Tree 206
Now is the time for Africa 207
Only a Phone Number 209
The God of the Impossible 210
The Ultimate Goal 213
Yunus Comes to the Lord 216
One of Christ's Trophies 217

XI Meeting Practical Needs

A God Idea 223
Bringing Christ to the Drug Pits of Madrid 225
Food, Fun and Faith 226
Serving as a Dentist 227
The Zawadi challenge 229

XII God Provides

A Home on the Mountain 233
God is Able 235
Never Had a Big Bank Account 236
Can I trust God to Provide without my Help? 237
Unplanned Journey and Unimagined Blessings 239
God's Wonderful Supply 242

XIII God Hears and Answers Our Prayers

A Bottle with a Message 247
Darkness is as Light to God 248
Angels to the Rescue 250
Little Bright Eyes 252
Matters of Life and Death 253
Our Son's Birth 254
Rescue from a Burning Car 257
Resurrection Buns 259
Saved from the Congo Carnage 262
Overcoming Obstacles or Uphill Home 271
Victory at the Bridge 273
A Gem Sparkles in the Desert 276

XIV Short God Stories

Short God Stories 281
- A Bowl of Reese Puffs 281
- A Memorable Prayer Meeting 282
- A Toggle Switch 282
- Catching Garbage 283
- Fitness Class? 283
- Seed Brings Fruit in God's Time 283

Three Soldiers Came in my Bedroom 284
Trusting Neighbours in 1998 284
Trusting Neighbours in 2009 285

Note from the Editor

God is on the throne. Jesus is alive. The Holy Spirit is working. I hope many reading this book will be encouraged and motivated to answer his call, and that you will be inspired by the dedication and faith of WEC workers.

Gathering the stories to commemorate 100 years of Worldwide Evangelization for Christ in Canada has been a joy. I trust the various stories will speak to you. Two old men pulling a van up a steep muddy incline, as they make a statement to the powers of darkness; a fresh bottle of water in the salty sea, floating toward a thirsty missionary; angels in a bright red Land Cruiser coming to the rescue in the desert; and a young language student with resurrection buns presenting the Easter message to a class of unbelievers in a land hostile to Christianity; are just a few of the vivid pictures that will remain with me forever.

Marian den Boer

Preface

Then the angel showed me the river of the water of life, as clear as crystal, flowing from the throne of God and of the Lamb down the middle of the great street of the city. On each side of the river stood the tree of life, bearing twelve crops of fruit, yielding its fruit every month. And the leaves of the tree are for the healing of the nations. Revelation 22:1-2*

I have heard many missionary talks and read many prayer letters over the years, some have been excellent and some, not so good. The things that I remember a day, a week, or even years later are rarely the statistics or the well-worked-out ideas, but the stories. Jesus often taught using stories. Stories capture our imagination and continue to speak to us long after our initial exposure. True stories enlarge our vision as they tell of the humanity of the speaker and the mighty power of God working in their midst. The stories help build our faith, encouraging us and inspiring us to prayer and action.

We all have stories of God's working in our lives. At WEC (Worldwide Evangelization for Christ) Canada, we decided to capture some of these stories to celebrate God's working in and through WEC Canadian workers over the 100 years since WEC came to Canada in 1924. As we deliberated on a title for this book we were struck by how the Lord has called us to share in his great plan for the healing of the nations, that those in darkness might come to know our Lord of light. This brought to mind Revelation 22 where healing is brought about through leaves; we, as Canadians, in keeping with our flag, are like fragile but colourful maple leaves, which have been directed by the wind of the Spirit to many lands for the Lord to use in bringing his healing to the nations.

Our stories are not just about us or for us, they are meant to be shared to be a blessing for others, and we hope that they will inspire and encourage you to be a leaf born by the Spirit of God to go where he would send you.

Caroline Brown

**In this book, scripture references are from the New International Version (NIV) Zondervan 2011, unless otherwise indicated.*

WEC International in Canada - History

Following is a fairly accurate non-comprehensive chronological background of WEC activities in Canada. Special thanks to Jack Aitken and Walter Mohr for their research and notes that were used extensively, and to Anna Pikkert who organized our archive files.

1913: Beginnings of Worldwide Evangelization for Christ in United Kingdom.
1924: A Canadian crusade board and office are instituted after a visit by Priscilla Studd (C.T. Studd's wife). Rev. W.F. Roadhouse is involved.
1926: Muriel Harman joins WEC. She goes to DR Congo where she is martyred in 1964.
1928: Norman Grubb does four months deputation in Canada – this visit ultimately leads to the establishment of Inter-Varsity Christian Fellowship in Canada and the USA!
1932: Irene James joins WEC. Alfred Ruscoe has 10-month exploratory trip to Canada and USA.
1936: Alfred Ruscoe starts a sending base at 163 College St. Toronto Canada – the first not in the UK. (He had wanted to start in the USA but it was thought an Englishman would be better accepted in Canada!) The office is in a rented one room apartment, divided by a screen.
1937: Cyril Holloway, Gertrude Woods, Iva Crocker, Ethel Rodway, Horace Davey and family go to the field, most to start WEC's new work in Liberia.
1938: The first missionary to have all his orientation and acceptance in Canada is Ralph Hines, who goes to Colombia. *Ralph bookkeeps for Alfred in Canada before going to Colombia, where his son, Jon (Ralph) Hines is born. Jon later joins WEC Canada and serves as our treasurer (for over 30 years) until 2024.*
1938: Norman Grubb's second tour (10 months) in Canada and USA. Many

respond to the challenge of missions.

1939?: In Canada, Earl Frid starts the first all North American WEC newspaper.

1941: Reba Fleming, daughter of ex-Toronto mayor, purchases 11 Roxborough St E, Toronto, and invites WEC to be her guests in this 33-room house. *Later, a year before she dies, Reba donates $25,000 toward the purchase of a Canadian WEC headquarters.*

1946: Alfred Ruscoe opens a North American headquarters in the USA; Toronto/Canada becomes a branch. Edwin Gillman becomes leader of the Canada branch.

1951: Jack Cairns becomes Canadian leader until Earl and Ethel Frid are appointed later in the year. They leave Toronto because of a subway development and move to Beamsville (127, 133 and 149 King St.). Helpfulness of candidates and others to a neighbouring farmer results in decades of fruit supplies for WEC staff and candidates.

1952: Kae Johnston, June Louise Frid, Elsie Hopkins and Miles Sim sail to Pakistan together. Helen Krueger and Adeline Wilke pioneer Muslim outreach in Côte D'Ivoire.

1959: Earl Frid wins Supreme Court challenge, WEC is recognized as a seminary and granted tax exemption in Canada. *Note: this status is not carried over to 37 Aberdeen until Rick Jones moves us to apply.*

1963: Alfred and Ellen Ruscoe return to lead WEC in Canada and move headquarters back to Toronto, purchasing 144 High Park Avenue.

1966-71: Briefly Harold and Willa Holder but then, Gordon and Gwyneth Gale lead WEC in Canada. Canadian candidates continue to be trained in the USA at the North America headquarters.

1968: Elwin Palmer is appointed WEC North American leader in USA.
Mollie Norton opens Cherith House as "a home for missionaries on furlough" at 944 Owenwood Drive, Mississauga.

1971-75: Clarence and Lucille Knapp are appointed leaders in Canada.

1975: WEC Canada reborn as an independent WEC sending base with Ken and Racile Getty as leaders.

1976: 37 Aberdeen Ave. is purchased to be WEC Canada's headquarters.

1977: First Canadian WEC annual conference is held August 21-26.

1979: Dan and Mary* go to Jordan, then United Arab Emirates, the start of many Canadians joining WEC's work with Muslims in the Middle East.

1980: Peter* expresses interest in working with Kurds and joins WEC Canada to pioneer that work.

1981: First candidate orientation wholly in Canada since 1951.

1984: David* joins WEC, becomes our first worker in Kazakhstan.

1980's: WEC purchases another building in Hamilton to house staff – mortgage paid off in 3 years. In these years WEC Canada sponsors a new work in Fiji.

1990: Canadian WECers help start Bible school in Equatorial Guinea.

1992: Philip and Nancy Wood become WEC Canada leaders (until 2001); Ken and Racile Getty go to British Columbia (BC).

1995: Purchase of property and establishment of Gateway Cross-Cultural Training Centre in Langley, BC (opens in 1996).

2001: Third Hamilton staff housing property bought; is later sold but then another bought in 2019.

2002: Henry and Nancy Bell become WEC Canada leaders (until 2011).

2009: Land of Goshen property is donated to WEC for potential Betel (addictions) ministry and extensive renovations and expansion work take place.

2011-13: Interim leadership team: Linda Nagel, Randy and Heather Barnes, Walter and Melita Mohr.

2013-26 Mick and Caroline Brown are the WEC Canada leaders.

2019: Gateway property sold; leaders, Mike and Laurie Boling, move to Hamilton and start C.O.M.E. program.

2026: Colin and Miranda Meikle become WEC Canada leaders.

* Last names withheld

I

Seeds

Sow your seed in the morning, and at evening let your hands not be idle, for you do not know which will succeed, whether this or that, or whether both will do equally well.
Ecclesiastes 11:6

WEC missionaries know that the Word of God has to be sown in hearts for it to germinate and multiply. They don't know where or when or which seed will sprout. They just know to plant the seed as the Lord directs.
Whether the Holy Spirit uses a giant bunch of holly on a bus, a riddle about valleys and ditches, a guitar, or a Muslim holiday celebration, he is creative in the opportunities he provides to plant those seeds.

Sharing with a Busload of People

Karli in the Middle East, 2016

I bought a small bunch of those silly prickly green leaves with red berries on them because my mom likes them and I wanted to surprise her with a present. The gypsy lady I buy flowers from is my friend as I often stop to visit with her, so she added five more bunches of holly as a present to me. Suffice to say I looked rather silly walking down the street with this giant bunch of flowers.

Suddenly, a city bus stopped beside me, even though I wasn't anywhere near the bus stop. The elderly bus driver yelled out, "Your flowers are beautiful! Hop on." He was so excited about my flowers he gave me a free ride and put my flowers behind his steering wheel so he could enjoy them while he drove. He started talking to me even though it's forbidden for drivers to let people on the bus when they are not at a stop, to give free rides and to talk to the passengers. He was extraordinarily cheerful and animated.

There were a lot of people on the bus. I was somewhat in shock. Anyway, he went on to ask me if I was from the Black Sea because my eyes were green. He was from the Black Sea. I explained I was not and that I was actually a foreigner. He happily whipped out a picture of his foreigner friend and asked me if I knew him. I didn't, but I asked the driver if his friend was a Christian. He said no, but then he launched into a big discussion about Jesus and he asked if I had read the holy books.

The driver was super hungry to hear more and I ended up sharing my testimony and the gospel. Also, everybody who got on the bus loved my flowers so much they all wanted to stay at the front of the bus to enjoy them and the driver was talking so loudly many people heard our conversation. I was feeling shy and awkward but also overjoyed. Then he asked me to send him verses about Jesus from the gospel.

And I thought the green prickly leaves and red berries weren't worthy to be called flowers!

A Prayer Walk

Esther in the Middle East, 2004

One day I felt led to prayer walk in a neighbouring city. Perhaps God was calling me to live and work there. During my prayer walk, I encountered two ladies completely covered in black. Even their eyes and hands were covered. Only their feet poked out. They asked me what I was doing and I told them I was going for a walk and they were welcome to join me if they could keep up. I am tall compared to the local people and the ladies there tend to glide along very differently to the way we walk in the west. They agreed to join me. We walked along the seashore and all the while I told them about Jesus and my faith in him. After an hour we returned to where we had started and they went on their way to do their shopping in the city centre.

A year later God did call me to work in that city. I hadn't taken the ladies names or phone numbers so I had no idea who or where they might be. Then three years later, a fellow worker told me about meeting a local lady. This local lady had mentioned that several years previously, she had met a tall English woman walking who had told her about Jesus. Now she wanted to know more about Jesus and find out more about the Bible.

Amazing! God leads us to people who are ready to hear his truth. He simply asks us to be faithful to share him with those we meet. We are all links in a chain leading to Jesus, the anchor.

The Valley and the Ditches

Walter Mohr in Indonesia, 1960's

Make the valley full of ditches. 2 Kings 3:16

God's word came to Elisha while a harpist was playing, and that same word came to me repeatedly, waking me up early morning after morning and leaving a deep impression. Melita and I had been in Java Indonesia for only 15 months. We were not yet totally fluent in the language but the command was compelling. Make the valley full of ditches. What could it mean? What should I do?

The valley was fertile—the rice fields in the valley as well as those stretching upward in neat terraces were growing well. The sugar cane was also thriving. Indeed, we were living in a lush valley. Looking to the west I saw Mt. Lawu and to the east was Mt. Willis. But hearts were hard. The calls from every mosque reminded every man, woman and child that there is no God but Allah and his prophet was not Jesus.

But God's word came with such force that I wrote it in my diary, I also wrote it on a notepad that I was keeping as I prayed. As I pondered the command in our context it seemed to mean, make channels through which living water can flow. But how was this to happen?

The obvious ditch was God's word and the gospel message. But how could those channels be made? The vision took shape—we needed to saturate the valley with the good news. We needed to sow the seed far and wide. It became our passion. We visited every village market we found. We sold thousands of books and Bibles. We gave out untold thousands of tracts. We advertised a short free correspondence course. We preached in the markets, at roadsides and wherever people gathered. Using flip charts attracted attention. Some young people responded and believed. Some caught the vision and took the good news to more distant villages. Ditches were being dug all over the valley. Much seed fell on hard ground and never did sprout but some also fell on good ground and began to grow.

Three years later a failed communist coup brought untold suffering and death. Great fear gripped many hearts. The trickle coming to faith became a river. Books sitting on shelves were opened again and reread. Dreams led some to search for truth. The heavens were open and living water was flowing widely. Bondages were broken. Charms were burned. The Holy Spirit brought conviction. Lives were changed. Believers invited neighbours and friends. House churches sprang up where Christ's name had never been known. Local churches were organized and elders were appointed. The church was growing despite the rise of opposition. We were reliving the New Testament.

Opposition and persecution grew. But the message was powerful and the living water was life-giving. What God was doing in our valley He was also doing in other valleys. The dew from heaven was filling the land. Indonesia witnessed something remarkable and unstoppable. People spoke of it as a revival. Books were written about it. The promise became a reality. Streams from heaven filled the land.

Following that Still Small Voice

Josh in the Middle East, 2023

Just as the cold and snow was beginning to fall over much of the country, we set out to fit in one last outreach trip before taking a break for the winter. We visited a major city in the southeast of the country, an area known for its incredible hospitality culture. Hospitality comes with conversations over cups of tea and with those conversations come natural opportunities to share the good news.

On this trip, while there was all the usual hospitality and opportunities to sit and talk, there was an unusual hesitancy to talk about deeper things. The city had suffered from various political movements, most recently in 2015, resulting in weeks of bombings and gunfights in the streets—we could still see walls pockmarked with bullet holes. In this country, religion is closely tied to politics, national identity, and race; consequently many were justifiably hesitant to talk about religion with strangers. Despite the general nervousness on the subject, we did manage to have a few good conversations and leave some books and Bibles.

One night while we were sitting in a coffee house with live traditional music, a young man requested a song to be dedicated to his wife for their first anniversary. I felt strongly that I should pay his bill and attempted to do so without him noticing. I almost got away, but he managed to catch me and thanked me. The next day we were visiting a Dengbej house—a place set up for traditional storytellers who tell modern and historical stories by singing them in Kurdish.

While we were sitting listening, who should come in but the guy whose bill I had paid the night before! We nodded at each other from across the room. Later we met outside, briefly talked and exchanged information. He told me he was from another city but came because he loved Dengbej. A few days later I remembered a Dengbej Gospel of John was available online. I sent my friend the link.

While we haven't been able to talk in much depth so far, I believe there must be a reason I felt the sudden need to pay his bill and happened to meet him again the next day in a city of well over a million. I don't know what the Lord has planned, but I trust and pray that the Lord will use this to stir his heart and draw him near.

Only a Mustard Seed of Confidence

A Worker in the Middle East, 2018

God was asking me to reach out to the Pashtun people. I studied and learned the language, then prayed God would guide me to a Pashtun family. A month went by and I almost gave up hope of finding a Pashtun friend. I had asked everyone I knew to look around, but this city is so massive it was like finding a needle in a haystack. That day I was cooking curry and the recipe called for mustard seeds. By accident I spilled them on the floor and noticed how tiny they were. Then I sat down to read my Bible and it opened right to the parable of the mustard seed. I read it and was soon encouraged. I felt the Holy Spirit telling me that I should have a mustard seed of confidence that the Lord knew where to find Pashtuns in this city. I knelt to pray and immediately I received a text from a friend to say she had found a Pashtun family.

The Pashtun woman cried when I walked in her door to greet her in her own language. This was a refugee family, a mother with seven children threatened with deportation. After several visits, which would last for hours, the mother said, "I no longer want to be a Muslim." She had been reading the Bible I had left with her. A few weeks later, half of the family made the decision to follow Christ. My heart is bursting with excitement about what God is doing in this family.

Only the Holy Spirit Knows

Fred in the Middle East, 2023

I regularly go out in search of possible converts in areas in the city where there are no known churches or believers, so when I heard about a concert featuring a famous singer, I decided to go. I knew a lot of unreached people would be at the concert. I arrived four hours early, so I wandered around the area. Some 500,000 people lived there on the outskirts of the city.

As I walked about, a particular building piqued my interest so I asked a random guy on the sidewalk about it. He said it was a factory of some sort. After meeting, we strolled together for a bit. He said that he had just spent several years in jail for murdering someone. He carried guilt and shame and didn't know how he could ever be forgiven. He had never met a Christian before. I was able to share how Jesus could forgive him and save him. He wanted a Bible and I was able to pray with him. I hope he became a believer but I'm not sure—only the Holy Spirit knows.

Planting Seeds at an Eid Kabir Celebration

Leah in North Africa, 2019

I lived overseas once before—in Madagascar during my college internship—which in no way prepared me for the diversity in beliefs found in this country in North Africa. I had studied Islam and its beliefs, but hadn't factored in the unique political history and geographical location which play a big part in the values and beliefs of the young people here. Islam in this country is not just tied to religion; the culture and social interaction depend on it. A person is a Muslim whether they believe or follow the religious laws or not.

My first year in the country was the loneliest year I have ever experienced. I didn't know the language very well and I didn't have much interaction with other expatriates, but God blessed me with one local girl I can truly call my friend. I will call her Rachel. I believe Rachel was a direct gift from God. I met her on the bus nearly two years ago and we have been friends ever since. She is one of the most conservative Muslims I have ever met. Her whole family are devout followers of Islam. I have had numerous conversations with her about Jesus, but I would like to share one that stands out.

I had been invited to Rachel's house to celebrate Eid Kabir with her family. This is the big holiday when they remember the day Abraham went to the mountain to sacrifice his son for the Lord (they believe it was Ishmael, not Isaac). In remembrance of the occasion, each family sacrifices a sheep and afterwards, celebrates with an enormous feast. After watching all the gory details, the family asked me what I thought of the whole process.

I was very nervous; but I had prayed for this opportunity. I shared the story of the great sacrifice. I could see that I had the room's attention, especially that of the father. I knew that if I wanted to see the whole family come to Jesus, ideally, I would want the father to accept him first. As I shared the story, I could tell that my words were difficult for the father to swallow. We talked back and forth for nearly an hour, and then one of his sons asked about the bottom line—where our salvation ultimately comes from.

I also got to hear their view of sin and where they put their hopes. We talked about issues of the heart and how in the end Jesus Christ is the only person who can heal and remove our struggles and addictions. I do believe something divinely spiritual happened that day. This family, for the first time in their life, had a chance to hear the gospel from an actual believer. For years, even from birth, they have believed many misconceptions about our beliefs. I pray that something I said stuck with them, that their hearts are prepared to accept Jesus.

Small Seeds

Karen at WEC Canada Headquarters, 2024

Again, he said, "What shall we say the kingdom of God is like, or what parable shall we use to describe it? It is like a mustard seed, which is the smallest of all seeds on earth. Yet when planted, it grows and becomes the largest of all garden plants, with such big branches that the birds can perch in its shade." Mark 4: 30-32

Lately, I have been wondering about the eight years spent in our country of service in Central Asia. My husband and I did not see anyone come to the Lord—never led anyone to personal salvation in Christ. It's hard to admit this. Every missionary wants to see souls saved and a church planted but not all of us get to do that. It has been embarrassing at times. It's taken time to learn and accept that my ways are not his ways and to trust the Lord knew what he was doing in sending us there. I've asked him to bring to my mind the little things that meant something. In thinking on this, I am reminded of the passage about small seeds, mustard seeds.

It is my eternal hope and prayer that all the little seeds we planted, in word or deed, will grow to be giant trees flourishing for his kingdom and that maybe one soul will turn the tide in his or her village and spread the good news.

The seeds that come to mind are very small and seem insignificant on their own but as I think on them, I see the faces and reactions of those receiving them. They look bewildered, confused, then thankful. When we left, we knew we had a month to pack up and go. Dissolving our house and all our stuff was so sad for me. It was my first time living in a house with a yard, not an apartment. It was especially dear to me that the house was new and therefore empty and so for the first time in my married life I personally furnished and decorated my home. I made all the choices and wasn't stuck with old, mismatched, too-big furniture and full cupboards. So, parting with things along with being forced to leave, was very hard. We weren't done God. What are you doing?

I gave my sewing machine to a local believer who was thrilled to care for it should I return. I donated a box of English books to the local library where patrons go to read books—not to borrow. I can still see the look of amazement on the librarians' faces when I said I was gifting them all those books. I imagine they swarmed the box the moment I was gone. I don't remember which books we gave but there were more than a few Christian ones among them. Who has read those books, Lord? Most of the people we met there, love to learn English and are very good at it.

I asked a family we were close to if they would care for a box of our favourite books, in case we return some day. Not long after we left, the mom shared with me that the box included a kids' devotional book in the local language. They read it together every night and are learning all about Jesus and the Bible.

We had a pile of gospel literature hiding in our house. We needed to get rid of it fast. No one else had room to store all of it. So, we began to go for long drives, stopping here and there to leave a pamphlet or book or CD sitting on a bench or at a bus stop, knowing that someone would pick it up, read it and maybe pass it on. We prayed as we went, asking God to show us where to stop and to bless each item that we left. Who found them Lord? Did our seeds get a chance to take root, to grow? We also gifted a box of craft supplies to the local Girl Scouts club. The lady leading the troop had accepted Christ through a coworker. This coworker and I had a small ladies club where a handful of women had permission to come visit with us, cook and do crafts. Did that matter Lord?

Earlier that year, another missionary handed out audio bible machines (like little handheld radios) with wind-up battery mechanisms. These devices allowed people to hear the gospel in the local language and were especially appreciated by older people who had never learned to read. In that culture, the only men I was allowed to speak with when I was alone were the older taxi drivers. In our village, we had one man we affectionately called Tahir Baba (Tahir Grandpa). I would phone him and he would come to take us shopping. One day I gave him the audio bible and suggested he listen to it when he was waiting in his car with nothing to do. He was very grateful. I don't know if he ever used it. Where did it end up Lord? Did it matter?

Another time, we were able to visit a neighbour and express condolences to the family on the death of a relative. What words could we offer them? I gave them a book of Psalms in their language. I told them that the psalms are always a comfort to me in hard times. I read them a psalm. A while later the young daughter-in-law shared with me that she was reading the book and enjoying it. I was a busy homeschool mom with two young girls. I regret not visiting her more and reading with her. Where is she Lord?

Lately, even on this side of the globe, we've seen glimmers of fruit from our seeds. Thanks to modern technology we remain in contact with a few local friends and there are signs of green growth poking through the soil. One friend messaged me on Facebook to say she has a new cleaning lady who "believes like you do." My prayers were answered that God would bring someone new into her life to keep sharing with her. I suspect the Bible that I gave her sits on the shelf of honour next to her Koran, rather than open in her hands. Now I pray for the cleaning lady and for more sharing to happen.

Last month my husband received a text from an old coworker. He shared that he ran into one of the boys that they used to teach basketball. The young man requested my husband's contact information. They are now communicating—discussing a dream this young man dreamed and specifically what religion means to us.

Two months ago, I received friend requests on Facebook, from the children of the only woman with whom I shared the whole gospel. The woman had been very resistant. Her children are adults now and I accepted their friend requests. I quickly found out that the brother is now an exchange student in the USA. With a bit of searching, I am able to tell from posts and pictures that he is staying with a Christian family. Go God! Save this young man, Lord. Send him back home full of you.

I am encouraged that our Heavenly Father called another family to our mission field. This family lives there, in a small village. They are the only believers along with one new local friend. The husband had a dream about our family, back when he was single and living in the USA. He told us that through this dream the Lord called him to our field. He first came as a single short termer and even babysat our kids a few times. The interesting part, and this is the part I love about the WEC Family, is he was a missionary kid in Mexico when I served there as a single woman. I know his family well. He and his wife went to our field about the time we were leaving. We passed the torch without trying.

God is gracious in all he does. Little by little he does his work, in ways unbeknownst to us, growing those tiny little seeds into tall, strong trees. May his name be praised. I pray he continues to grow my faith as well.

Worshipping in the Marketplace

Velm in South Asia, 2017

B*ut the hour is coming and now is, when the true worshippers will worship the Father in spirit and truth; for the Father is seeking such to worship him. John 4:23,24*

A certain nearby shop owner came to my mind while I was in prayer with some friends. I had visited him a number of times but some time had passed since I had seen him. Sensing this as a prompt from the Lord, I responded in my heart by asking the Lord to give me the opportunity to meet him if that's what the Lord wanted.

After our prayer time, a friend and I approached the shop and lo and behold there was the owner, waiting to see us. He called us in for tea and we caught up. Then he asked us to play a song or two on the guitar we had with us. We felt the Lord in this and broke out into worship. As soon as we started singing, we experienced God's presence in an amazing way. My friend was sweating on the strings and I was singing from my depths, eyes closed and lost in his love.

When I opened my eyes, I noticed that the shop was filling up. Our worship had attracted a number of bystanders. I did a bit of translating, explaining what and why we were singing. It was an amazing experience and our friend the shop owner couldn't get enough. We played on for a while and departed saying we expected to be back. I left ecstatic with a childlike joy in the bliss of this relationship with God.

My heart cries that these people will personally experience his grace and the presence of his Holy Spirit. I am praying for more opportunities like this and want to learn some contextual songs in the local language.

II

Divine Encouragement

Be strong, and let your heart take courage, all you who wait for the Lord!
Psalm 31:24

The Lord is always ready with a divine touch. In the following stories he speaks to a secret believer to encourage her to make her faith public; with the simple gift of two street car tickets he takes Verna Becker a very long way; he lovingly gives Caroline Brown a reality check when it comes to the value of her prayers; and in "Life Comes from Above," he uses a dream to renew Linda Nagel's faith in a long-awaited promise. God is faithful.

Jesus Speaks

Joy in the Middle East, 2023

We have a close friend who has faith but has never been bold enough to publicly show others what she believes. We have known her for eleven years. Recently she lost her home in the earthquake. Then in a dream, she saw a man dressed in shining white. She spoke to him and realized that she was speaking with the Lord Jesus.

She began to ask why he had not come and spoken to her before. Jesus said, "Oh, but I have been speaking to you for many years. I have been speaking to you through my servants. Who do you go to when you are crying? Who do you go to when you need help? Who do you ask to pray for you? When you go to my servants, I am there speaking to you through them." The servants Jesus was speaking about are the WEC workers in her city. This lady has now decided to be baptized. Praise the Lord that he is at work in this tragedy drawing people to himself and increasing the faith of many.

Two Streetcar Tickets

Verna Becker, WEC Headquarters in Toronto, 1940's

Living a life of faith and trusting God for every detail was a challenge. On one occasion I was asked to attend a meeting across the city of Toronto on behalf of WEC. The practice at that time was that when assigned to a meeting, we could pick up the necessary streetcar tickets at the office. However, I felt challenged that if I was trusting God to take me across the ocean to minister in Africa once my training was complete, I could at least trust him to take me across Toronto.

I was all dressed and ready to leave for my meeting, and at that point still had not received the money I would need to take the streetcar. Then just before I needed to leave for the meeting, I picked up my mail and was delighted to see five letters. Excitedly I opened the letters, beginning with those from home and from friends who had sent me money previously, but no money. Then I opened the last letter from a friend who was also living by faith. She was in mission work in a little place called Smoky Lake, Alberta and had no money herself, so you can imagine my excitement and surprise when I opened her letter and out dropped two Toronto streetcar tickets with a note saying, "I've had these for two years since my training there and I feel these will do you more good than me."

This was God's perfect timing: that letter arrived just minutes before I had to leave. There were no airmail services or special deliveries then, but God timed the arrival of that letter in answer to my prayers and just in time to catch my streetcar. That experience changed my life, and my trust and faith in God, forever.

Powerful Pray-ers

Caroline Brown in the Middle East, 2007

There is often an expectation put on missionaries. Sometimes people will invite my husband and I for a meal and invite the friends and relatives who they want us to save, counsel or pray with about a need. It is an honour but an awkward and often unrealistic expectation. What if the conversations don't naturally open up with me, a complete stranger? Could I have done more? Maybe I'm not a very good missionary, or maybe that wasn't a door that the Lord was opening to me. There can be an assumption that the missionary's prayers are somehow more powerful than other prayers.

I struggle with prayer. How do I know the Lord's will? Sometimes I sense what the Lord wants me to pray but often I don't. Should I claim healing for a person, or pray for patience and comfort for one who is not going to see the desired answer?

The difficulty in knowing how to pray is intensified when it is in a second language. I was part of a small local church in a predominantly Muslim country. My co-workers prayed with great confidence in Jesus' name giving assurance that the Lord would give the hoped for victory, healing, guidance, or employment. Their prayers seemed confident, fluent, and inspiring. One co-worker, who indeed was very spiritual and deeply versed in the scriptures, and a great worship leader (yet another thing I couldn't do), would place her hands over the person she was praying for with a dramatic trembling motion.

You had the sense that here was a powerful woman of God.

My prayers in contrast were quiet, my local language ability was stumbling, and I lacked the confidence to claim dramatic things. I didn't like to be called upon to pray in public, or even for individuals in a more private setting. One Sunday at the end of the church service I turned around to chat with the local believers behind me. One young lady confided she had had a difficult week and, after sharing some details, asked me to pray for her. I felt a sudden panic and wanted to suggest that she go and ask one of the church leaders or other prayer giants, but I knew I shouldn't. I don't remember what I prayed but I'm sure that I thanked God for his great love for this lady and prayed that she would know more of Jesus' love and presence in the coming week, as those are some things I can confidently pray for anyone going through difficult times. I was glad to be able to bring my simple and hopefully understandable prayer to an end and hoped she wasn't too disappointed in my stumbling prayer.

A week or two later the same young lady came to me and thanked me profusely; she said how encouraged she had been by my prayer and felt that the Lord had indeed been so much closer and was helping her through the difficulties. I was surprised and encouraged. I learned in practice what I knew in theory. It is not the person praying that is powerful, not even the prayers uttered, but our God is the powerful one. Also, I felt my Lord's gentle but firm rebuke, that my hesitancy to pray with others may be denying them an opportunity to be blessed by him.

Life Comes from Above

Linda Nagel in Côte d'Ivoire, 1980's

I battled discouragement. Had God not promised, through his word, and through visions, dreams and prophecy that his living church would be built in Boko? Questions swam through my head. Was the vision real? I did know that allowing negative thoughts a place in our minds opens doors to enemy attack. It wasn't until after I suffered two serious bouts of malaria that I awoke to my mistake. It's fatal to allow Satan a place in our thoughts. He is the accuser of believers and delights in emphasizing our weaknesses.

Early one morning while walking for exercise, I saw the sun just peeking over the horizon spreading a mellow glow over the mountains. A verse came to mind, *"Lift your eyes to the hills where your help comes from. Your help comes from the Lord who made the heavens and the earth."* It was about time I turned my eyes from myself and onto Jesus. As I walked, I considered him and the positive things he was doing.

That same week Mory, a relatively new believer, stopped to visit. "I had a very interesting dream last night," he said. "I saw the Barala people streaming down the mountainside into the marketplace carrying Bibles. It looked like they were coming to a church conference." This vision was the same one God gave me ten years earlier. I hadn't shared it with the church or Mory. He was not repeating something he heard from me. God revived the vision and gave me courage to believe and to keep sharing Jesus. He assured me that he would fulfill the vision in his time.

Even with the assurance that God would answer prayer and bring fruit in his time, I still laboured in my heart and believed I had to do more to fulfill God's promise. One night, I woke up around two thirty in the morning and started thinking about Mamadou (our house helper) and how long he's been with us and how much of the gospel he knew. Yet he still had not accepted Christ. I tossed and turned mulling over my failures.

To get my mind off myself, I started praising the Lord and promptly fell asleep. I had a dream. I was with my Muslim Outreach Team colleagues. I saw two poles stuck in the ground, like short telephone poles. We struggled to pull them up, trying to force them to grow. Little by little they became taller, but there was no life in them. They remained dead wood. Frustrating. As we contemplated what to do next, two hands came down from the clouds carrying leafy tops of palm trees. The hands grafted these into the tops of the poles. The poles then became alive. A co-worker was with me in the dream. As we watched the poles become living trees we sat back and laughed with relief. All our struggles were in vain. Life couldn't come through our human efforts. Life comes from above.

Beyond the Mud *(2015) by Linda Nagel, pages 164-5, 177-8.*

III

Answering the Call

Then Jesus came to them and said, "All authority in heaven and on earth has been given to me. Therefore, go and make disciples of all nations, baptizing them in the name of the Father and of the Son and of the Holy Spirit, and teaching them to obey everything I have commanded you. And surely, I am with you always, to the very end of the age."
Matthew 28:18-20

Imagine you have an overwhelming fear of snakes, even harmless common garter snakes and then you are called to a country in Africa where venomous snakes abound. In this country garter snakes are dangerous and cobras, mambas and vipers thrive. What do you do?
Sometimes answering the sure, clear call to missions is a matter of overcoming fear, and sometimes it means turning your back on a materially promising and comfortable life. Sometimes answering the call leads to martyrdom.
Often the call is clarified with a short-term mission trip. A call can come anytime during a lifetime as Rick Jones attests. For some, becoming a missionary is the path to personally meeting Jesus. God works in many unpredictable ways when it comes to the great commission.

Called to Africa

Linda Nagel, 1960's

"How did you know that God called you to Africa?" asked a friend recently. Here's my story.

It happened during a slide presentation on Ivory Coast (Côte d'Ivoire), in a little church in Nanaimo. A thought came very clearly into my mind, "You will see all those places one day." Sounds pretty simple doesn't it, but was this really from God? Maybe it was my imagination.

In the following weeks I picked up a Readers Digest and there was a story about Ivory Coast, West Africa. The National Geographic came and it had an article titled "Ivory Coast, Africa's Success Story." Before this I hardly knew the country existed and now it hit me from every side.

The presenter of the slides was Hazel Grace McLean. Hazel had returned to Canada from Africa the previous year and was now pastoring a small church on Salt Spring Island. It was the same church my friend Joyce and I pastored before moving to Nanaimo to take up the youth ministry in a church.

After the meeting, my curiosity about Ivory Coast or Côte d'Ivoire couldn't be quenched. I had to have more talks with Hazel. I had to know more about the country and what it was like to be a missionary. Joyce and I paid her a visit on Salt Spring. "Why are you asking all these questions?" Hazel asked. "I don't know." I replied, "but I'm so drawn to that place."

Hazel also told me about WEC, the faith mission under which she had been serving. WEC's principle of living by faith and trusting the Lord alone to supply every need, was how I lived.

While talking with her I remembered another WEC missionary I met while attending Bible School, Kae Johnston. Her testimony, shared with the students, also left a great impression on me. My visit with Hazel affirmed what I was already thinking, "If I join a mission, it will be WEC."

But a struggle was going on in my heart. I had many arguments about why I should let the idea of missions drop, especially the part about serving in Africa; after all I had a terrible fear of snakes! But Africa would not leave my mind. Finally, after weeks of soul searching, and meditating on verses of scripture God brought to my attention, I said, "Lord if you want me to go to Africa, I will go." Peace flooded my soul. There was no doubt after that. This was God's will for me.

I wrote to my family in Alberta and told them I was applying to WEC to be a missionary to Africa. They were very supportive. Serving God was a high priority on their list of desires for their children. They saw it as an honour to have a child become a missionary, but it was still a wrenching experience for them when I actually left home for WEC USA.

WEC responded favourably to my application though I stated I couldn't go to the WEC headquarters for the candidate class before my sister's wedding which was the first week of November 1964. The course started in October.

When I think of my parents now, it must have been a hard time for them. My sister got married and left home with her new husband one day, and I left by train for Philadelphia the next.

I took all of my belongings because I thought that once I was accepted, I would be on my way to Africa for the next five years. Actually, following acceptance into the mission in 1965 I was free to return to Alberta that summer before going to French language school in Quebec in September.

During the candidate course at Camp Hill in Pennsylvania, I still struggled with the thought of Africa and whether I could cope with living in a country where snakes abound. The many snake stories missionaries seemed to delight in telling increased my fear.

One night in my room, shared with three other girls, candidates for other fields, I had a horrible dream. A big snake was chasing me and just as it opened its ugly mouth to shut on my trembling body I woke up. I don't know if I screamed but the quiet breathing of my roommates indicated their deep sleep had not been disturbed.

Still shaking, I began to pray and in my thoughts came this question, "Where did that dream come from?" I knew very well it did not come from the Lord and immediately into my mind flashed the verse, "*God does not give us a spirit of fear, but of power, of love and a sound mind.*"

Again, the question, "Then where did the dream come from?" Instantly I knew. Satan was sowing fear into my mind. Out loud, with the risk of others hearing, I declared, "Get out of here Satan. I rebuke this fear of snakes and will not allow it to keep me from doing God's will."

Instantly I felt calm and at peace. God removed the horrible paralyzing fear. I still don't like snakes but after that I didn't worry about them anymore. I was free to do what God had called me to do and go where He wanted me to go.

Proof of the deliverance came during a visit of my friend Joyce a few years after I arrived in Côte d'Ivoire. I was taking her to one of our stations in the forest when the car overheated while climbing a hill. I had to turn off the motor.

"Just stay here," I said. "There's a swamp at the bottom of the hill. I'll go see if I can get some water."

Out I jumped and walked into the tall grass that bordered the road. Joyce told me later she could hardly believe her eyes. She knew of my terrible fear of snakes when we lived together on Salt Spring Island, where there seemed to be an abundance of the creatures—and they were just garter snakes! I never walked into grass if I couldn't see a clear path ahead. Now I nonchalantly marched into the bush.

Soon I returned with the murky water, put it into the radiator and we were on our way.

Over the many years I served in Côte d'Ivoire, I faced far greater challenges than confronting snakes. In every challenge fear reared its ugly head but the experience of deliverance during those months at WEC headquarters came to my mind. If God gave me the strength to overcome once, he could do it again.

God does give us a clear call, but Satan will always challenge it. Thank God we have the victory in our Lord Jesus Christ, and yes, I did see all those places, just like he promised.

The Story of our Calling

Caroline Brown, 1996

I could stand in my living room and see across ranch land, to the foothills and beyond to the Rocky Mountains. This was our dream house, our acreage. We had moved from England a few years earlier as Mick had been offered a job in Calgary. Within a few months of our arrival, we had moved onto our acreage, 20 kilometres outside of the city. We didn't come to the land of wide-open spaces to live in a city. Here our two children were born, we had two dogs, two cats, chickens, ducks and sheep, and five garages. Here we were happy, content. Mick's work was going well, our children were thriving, we were active members of our church and I volunteered at a hostel for the homeless.

But then we started to have a niggling feeling. I think it stemmed from praying, which just goes to show that you should be careful about praying. It was as if God was saying, "Are you willing to give all this up for me and go to those who have never heard?" Of course, we knew the right response and responded with the correct answer, "Of course, Lord, if you say so." But surely, he didn't really mean it, he was just seeing if we were willing. It would have made so much more sense years earlier before we were married, before we had a home, children and responsibilities. We had asked God when we had finished our science doctorates at Oxford while we were still only engaged to be married, and at that time he had said no—so why now?

Yet, the questions kept coming. Are you willing to give up your dream home? Are you willing to put aside the security and independence of a paid job and depend on me for your needs? Are you willing to lose out on a western health service and education for your children? Will you make me wait until you have a third child and then wait until he/she is old enough to travel? Slowly, painfully I/we wrestled with these questions and came to a point of submission before the Lord, still hoping that at that point, he'd respond, "Good, just wanted to know you were willing, now you can stay." But no, the final question came, "Now, will you go?" and we said yes. Someone asked us how two such logical people could do something so illogical but when the all-knowing Lord of the universe, who loves us infinitely and knows what is best, asks us to go, how could we refuse.

There was no doubt, we were going overseas, long-term. But we didn't know where, or to do what, or with whom. We felt the unfairness of so many millions of people in lands where the chances of their ever meeting a follower of Jesus were almost zero. Cities much larger than Calgary had no churches, no fellowships of believers, and maybe just a few isolated believers. It was right that God should send people to them.

But where was God asking us to go? Having asked us to go, he was now silent. We began talking to different mission agencies. They asked us where we wanted to go. What a stupid question, we wanted to stay where we were on our acreage with our dogs, but even more than that we wanted to know where God wanted us to go.

Agencies asked us to list our preferences...somewhere not too hot, not too big a city, preferably somewhere I could still speak English (I found language learning difficult), maybe I could be a teacher at an international school for MKs (missionary kids)—they are always short of science teachers. One agency suggested Chiang Mai in Thailand, they said it was in the mountains and not too hot and I could teach at the MK school, and Mick could learn the language and be involved in teaching locals. Sounded great but God gave no confirmation—silence.

We were given a book by one agency, *Tinker, Tailor, Missionary?* by Michael Griffiths. As we read it, it challenged many of our preconditions and confirmed what God had laid on our hearts. God wanted us to go where the gospel was least known, to learn the language and live among the people. Then there was a poem in the book. Mick read it first, then he read it to me.

Obedience

By George MacDonald

(1824-1905)

I said: "Let me walk in the fields."
He said: "No, walk in the town."
I said: "There are no flowers there."
He said: "No flowers, but a crown."

I said: "But the skies are black;
There is nothing but noise and din."
And He wept as He sent me back –
"There is more," He said; "there is sin."

I said: "But the air is thick,
And fogs are veiling the sun."
He answered: "Yet souls are sick,
And souls in the dark undone!"

I said: "I shall miss the light,
And friends will miss me, they say."
He answered: "Choose tonight
If I am to miss you or they."

I pleaded for time to be given.
He said: "Is it hard to decide?
It will not seem so hard in heaven
To have followed the steps of your Guide."

I cast one look at the fields,
Then set my face to the town;

He said, "My child, do you yield?
Will you leave the flowers for the crown?"

Then into His hand went mine;
And into my heart came He;
And I walk in a light divine,
The path I had feared to see.

It hit home. We both fell quiet. We said to one another, do you think God is telling us to go to that city? Months earlier a friend had invited us to join her in the work in her city in the Middle East, but we had dismissed it—a huge, crowded, polluted city, our friend got sick every winter and the summers were too hot. The people were unresponsive to the gospel. It was so dark and unattractive in our minds. Surely not there? But after reading the poem, we decided we should at least pray about it. We prayed, "Lord, if you want us to go there, we will go, but you are going to have to convince us because we don't want to go. Also, if we go there then we probably should go with WEC, and we don't like WEC either."

The next day we wrote a letter there (the old-fashioned way using pen and paper) to our friend in that city asking what Mick could do. It would be a couple of weeks before she received it, and we started to draft a letter to WEC. We never sent the letter because the following day, the second day after reading the poem, while Mick was at work, the phone rang. The caller introduced himself as Philip Wood, the Canadian director of WEC, calling from Hamilton. He didn't know who I was but phoned to say that he had been asked to send me a cheque by a worker in the Middle East and wanted to know why. I replied that it was probably because I distributed a newsletter for the WEC team in that country, and they had suggested they would send money for the postage, although I hadn't really expected any.

But then, since I unexpectedly had the director of WEC on the phone, I felt I had to act on what God was saying to us. I blurted out, "My husband and I feel that God is calling us to that country, and we don't want to go." When Philip asked why we didn't want to go, I told him it was crowded, polluted and opposed to the gospel. He told me how he had visited a few months earlier and described a very different viewpoint. That didn't sound too bad but still I wasn't convinced easily. I continued, "If we go there then we probably should go with WEC but I don't like WEC!" It was probably a bit rude to say that to the Canadian director of WEC but if I could make him close the door to us then maybe God would have to send us somewhere else, and with another mission. But Philip calmly asked why. I gave three specific reasons and he very graciously answered each. I began to think maybe I could work with this man and with this agency. I asked my final question, "But if we went there, what could we do? We can't go to a Muslim country with missionary stamped in our passports—maybe I could work as a science teacher in the MK school." Philip answered, "No, you are too young, you need to go and spend two years learning the language and culture, get alongside the local people and see what the Lord opens up for you." That sounded a lot like what God had been saying to us. Then Philip said, "I'm coming to Calgary in two months and I'd like to come and visit you." Wow, what coincidences, what timing!

That was the first of several amazing confirmations the Lord gave over the next few days. These included: an invitation in the mail to attend a network conference in the very same country; a verse of scripture that jumped out at me, where Paul is told on the Damascus Road, *"go into the city, and you will be told what you must do"* Acts 9:6; and a crescent moon and Saturn that looked a lot like the country's flag. By the end of the week, we both said, "Okay God, we get it, we are going there, with WEC, and you'll show us what we are to do after we learn some language."

A year and a half later, we were living in that big, crowded city. Our children were four and six years old. We lived in an apartment building, outside our windows were walls, more apartment buildings, shops, and lots of people and cars. But we were where God wanted us. We regularly took the ferryboat to get to language school and enjoyed the wonderful views of the water, the many seabirds, the historic sites, and tried out our few words of language with the other people on the ferryboat who wanted to talk to the foreigners with the cute children. It was the start of our 15 years in an amazing country.

God Affirms Jason's Call

Jason in the Middle East, 2017

Things finally came together. For three years, Jason dreamed of going to the country in the Middle East where God had called him. Because of numerous food allergies and a restricted diet, doubts arose in his thoughts, "How will I ever find the food I need to live there?"

Then God opened the door for a three-month trip to his dream country.

God did above and beyond what Jason expected. In Cairo passengers were told the connecting flight to the Middle East was cancelled. Hours of waiting ensued while the airline tried to find another route. Jason began a conversation with a young man waiting for the same flight. This young man who happened to speak English turned out to be from the country where Jason was heading. They talked and exchanged thoughts about their separate religions and beliefs. When the airline offered Jason a hotel room, he refused it because his friend did not qualify for the same service. Their friendship was cemented. Finally, a new flight was arranged and Jason and his new friend were on their way. His friend asked him many questions about his faith and Jason shared the message of salvation. At their destination, they exchanged phone numbers before parting.

Twice, Jason met up with his new friend. Conversations about Jesus continued. The young man didn't show an interest in following Jesus but Jason was excited to have a friend who could tell him about the country and culture and he delighted in studying the language.

He joined a group of new workers visiting various areas of the country. During that trip he learned how seasoned workers evangelized and he met more young nationals who spoke English. Although some showed interest in what Jason believed about Jesus and the Bible, it was discouraging to often hear, "Your book has been changed." In other words, it had no value.

The trip proved to Jason that when God calls, he also provides for all our needs. Jason didn't eat like he would have back home, but he found living in this country of service doable. He not only survived but gained weight while away.

After this trip Jason's call to long-term service in this Middle-Eastern country grew stronger than ever.

How I got into Missions

Kelly in North Africa, 2017

I was not born into a Christian home. Religion was a foreign thing in our high-achieving household. It was frowned upon. When I was 12, I began walking down a destructive, sinful path pursuing the world and its revelry.

In good timing, a friend invited me to join her youth group. I tagged along casually for a couple years, tuning out any spiritual talk and enjoying the fun and games. When I was 14, the youth group planned a retreat to a Bible camp in a beautiful forested area. I decided to join in and enjoy a weekend away with my friends. Once there, we were given an afternoon of solo time—a chance to retreat into nature to pray and read our Bibles. Frustrated, I wandered off into the trees, muttering to myself about how silly all this religion was and how I felt sorry for these people who were so deceived by it.

As I walked, I pulled a leaf off a tree and began to study it. I had never taken note of the intricacies of a leaf before—thousands of veins and lines on this one little leaf. And there were billions of them in this forest. I then noticed the same intricacies on my own hands. How could I have not taken note of these things before? In the most beautiful clearing in the woods, surrounded by astonishing creation, I stopped walking. My heart began to pound, and tears welled in my eyes as I realized that maybe I had been wrong. That maybe, God was real, and that he had made all of this, and that maybe he had made me. And if he made me, I could not live for myself anymore, but wanted to live for him.

Alone in that forest, I called out to Jesus to save me. It was as if God saw my hard, sinful heart, took it out, and put in a new one. I was transformed from the inside out. I was not looking for him, but he saw me walking on a path of death and reached down and grabbed me, as if to say, "No, *this is the way, walk in it!*"

After high school, I decided to follow the Lord's prompting and explore the possibility of missions. I headed overseas for a four-month, short-term placement and after two weeks of being there, I said to myself, "This is what I want to do for the rest of my life." Seeing firsthand the realities of those unreached by the gospel turned my world upside down, and I knew life in Canada could never be the same for me.

Walk With Me

Rick Jones with WEC since 1998

I grew up attending a mainline Christian church, going to Sunday school, and hearing Bible stories. By the time I reached my mid-teens, I was fed up with the hypocrisy and walked away. I began to live for self on a path of destruction involving criminal activities and womanizing, among other things.

One evening while in my early twenties, I strolled into a restaurant with my girlfriend on my right arm and my friend's girlfriend on my left arm (my friend was working that evening). There I spotted a rather beautiful young woman and thought, "She looks like she would be fun." My girlfriend introduced us. This girl happened to be a born-again, Bible-believing Christian who had been witnessing to my girlfriend. This intrigued me as I had never taken out a Christian girl before.

I called her the next day and asked to take her for a walk; she declined. I called several times throughout the next week, even using the excuse, "I have some questions about the Bible." She made it clear she wanted nothing to do with me. Now, I like a challenge, so I found out where she went to church, came in just before service, and boldly sat down beside her. The story is long and that day didn't end with a walk; rather, it concluded with a 45-minute car ride during which she spoke not a word. Let's just say, while I thought I had gone into that church to pursue a young lady, it turned out that God was pursuing me. I walked in to meet him. She was the instrument he chose to draw me to himself. She has taught me many things over the years; you see, that young lady soon agreed to be my wife and we have been together for more than 50 years.

Let me assure you, meeting God, and dating and marrying a godly woman changed my life. We started a family, had a boy and a girl, and we joined a solid Bible-preaching church. I found out that my wife had been to Bible college (I had no idea that those institutions even existed) and she knew more than I did. The husband is to be the head of the house (and she tried to defer to me in that role) but I had so much to learn.

In turn, our kids went to the same Bible college my wife had attended. I had, by this time, learned quite a bit through Bible study groups and serving in various positions in the churches (we moved a few times and had to start fresh with each new location). But now my kids knew more than I did and that's just not right so, at age 48, I told my boss I was leaving his employ to go to Bible college. To my great surprise, he wrote me a cheque to help with travel expenses. God blesses when you are walking on the path he sets before you. One of the main reasons I had to go to Bible college is that we, as a couple, wanted to respond to a call to missions and, while my wife was acceptable, I was not qualified.

We left a comfortable life with opportunities for advancement, and set aside three years. Twelve months later, I had a bachelor's degree in Biblical and General Studies. Now what? God had not shown us where he wanted us (or when or how or anything). "*Be still, and know that I am God*" came to mind, so I started towards a master's degree. During second year God led us to WEC International.

We have walked with WEC for more than 25 years, always under God's direction and always relying on his provision. My gifting is in administration and there was an opening for an administrator on the other side of the world in New Zealand. As this was where he was asking us to walk, we stepped out in obedience even though our kids complained that parents were not supposed to be the ones to leave. We were under-supported but God is faithful. A total stranger gave us a car to drive to church. That was one of several confirmations that we were on the right path.

When we returned to Canada (to attend to our daughter for medical reasons), we were offered the opportunity to serve at the Canadian headquarters. As we continued to walk the path set before us in obedience to his leading, he continued to bless. After five years, he guided us to leave a most fulfilling time and take up a new ministry in the west. In obedience, we drove out to Alberta where we began a prayer ministry. At one point we were travelling over 1,000 kilometres each month to lead or attend prayer meetings.

Our walk has solidified and we have had the absolute joy of bearing witness to his goodness over these many years. He has proved more than faithful, has blessed us beyond measure and it is our privilege to walk alongside others and help them as he leads. As an old song says, we are "Walkin' along, singin' a song, side by side."

Remembering My Husband - Pilot Don Collins

Shirley Collins Robertson in Liberia, 1969

Don and I had not set up any radio contact on January 12, 1969; after all it was just a routine flight. Later in the day, I knew something was very wrong when our office filled with missionaries and nationals all gathered at the radio transmitter. My heart sank. Somehow, I knew what I would hear and it was not the familiar sound of his airplane approaching the landing strip. I called the children into our bedroom to tell them something was wrong, and that we would have to be very strong and brave. I prayed with them before they went back outdoors.

Alone in the bedroom, I cried to God. Don had logged many hours on the plane; surely God would never let anything happen to him. Later that afternoon the sad news came. Our plane was gone and my husband was with Jesus along with two passengers, Nurse Hannah Schmidt and a Bassa lad. Tropical darkness fell indeed.

That Sunday evening as I sat in shock, I heard a knock. The door opened and one by one the elders, the evangelists, and all the dear Christians came in quietly, and sat with me in the stillness. No one spoke; some shed tears. How much it meant to me.

Before the funeral the next day I wept before the Lord and asked him to give me a word. As I read the Bible, the verse he gave me was the one our

Bible school had given Don's class in 1956. "Nay, *in all these things we are more than conquerors through him that loved us.*" I went to Don's funeral with the knowledge that God makes no mistakes. *"He doeth all things well."*

Never have I doubted God's call to Liberia. Those were wonderful years.

Travail, Triumph Jubilee *(1989) edited by Hellen J. Kuleskey, page 43.*

Melissa Meets Jesus

Melissa Swan in Chad 2020

For many years I thought I was a Christian, yet I had never actually met Jesus. I always strove to be good enough which is why I went to be a missionary in Africa. I had always tried to be a good daughter, a good wife, a good Christian and now I wanted to be a good missionary. I deliberately went to Chad, a place that looked really hard to live. Well, Chad melted my coping habits. My emotions no longer obeyed orders to hide. I was completely worn down after a few months. I felt like there was no light or breath in me. Jesus took me into missions so he could reach me. I asked God questions I hadn't asked him before.

"Why are you a good shepherd, but I only feel scorching heat and only eat dust and thorns? Where is the pasture?"

My Chadian friend told me, "I love Islam because I just need to follow the rules. I am never at a loss for what to do." Well, "me too!" I thought. What can I add to that. I tried to know and follow the truth, but I was dead inside. After 14 months, God brought us home to Canada and kept us here a while. There was a lot of healing and it was very painful. At many points along the way I had to turn towards him in order for him to continue his work in me.

One night I was reading the Bible to quiet the darkness and fears that kept me from sleep. I read for a while, then around midnight I started up the stairs to go back to bed. I heard a voice demanding acknowledgement, "Melissa." I had often heard this voice—demanding, knowing. This voice knew all my shortcomings, all my fears, everything I had done wrong, everything I tried to hide or get rid of that was still there inside me. This voice knew. He condemned me and he demanded I acknowledge him as my lord.

Then I heard a second voice. It called my name as well. The second voice was quiet and soft and gentle and I needed to choose. For the first time in my life, I had a choice and I chose the quiet voice. I chose Jesus. I had always wanted Jesus, but I hadn't known that I didn't have him. I went up the stairs and Jesus kept me safe from the hate-filled claws and glare of what I had rejected. Suddenly there was new life and infinite joy—all was bright and real in the centre of my soul where there had been dark unrest.

A few months later we went back to Chad. He wanted me to go with him. Jesus did. I had previously used religion to satisfy the darkness inside me and soothe and control my emotions, but now it was Jesus Christ in me and I felt very weak, but alive. The voices still yelled at the windows of my heart but they didn't dare step foot in me anymore.

The light and beauty of Jesus continues to heal and cleanse me inside. I used to feel like God's tool, only valuable as I was useful. Now I am his daughter, his bride and his work of art. My Muslim Chadian friends say, "You used to be always afraid. Now you are not."

I had known fear of darkness and uncontrollable terror in the hand of the God I knew was unsafe. I had been oppressed and brainwashed, spiritually abused to the point where all of myself felt evil. Everything else outside myself was God's goodness. That was my definition of God's goodness, just as my Chadian friends must never complain against their god whether he takes their children or causes death or illness. They must always be thankful to him. That's the kind of god I had served, not the true God.

Now I have experienced and actually felt his beauty and goodness. I feel loved and precious. I know that Jesus is stronger than the demons who scare my Chadian friends every day. When our baby was born in Chad a year after I was saved, his Chadian grandma was afraid of the evil eye when I commented on his growth. I was able to be confident and share that this baby, who we both loved, was born in the name of Jesus and is safe in that name just as I am safe, and just as my Chadian friends can be safe if they turn their faces to

Jesus and answer when he calls their name. Then they will discover that he is not just powerful. He is gentle and kind and will never sacrifice his children on the altar of his glory.

He walks with us in each sin-caused pain. Yes, Jesus reached into my heart. He took me to Chad as a missionary so he could save me.

Even during War God Makes a Way

Helen Krueger and Adeline Wilke in Côte d'Ivoire, 1945

Helen Krueger and Adeline Wilke, both from the Canadian prairies, met at the WEC headquarters in Toronto, Ontario. Both believed that God was calling them to the Belgian Congo and felt that He had called them to serve together.

While in candidate training, a WECer named Tom Fagan, home from the Côte d'Ivoire in West Africa, made an appeal for pioneer workers to reach the Muslim tribes of that country. Separately, God spoke to Helen and Adeline. Each one knew he was calling them to answer that call. But it was 1945 and World War 11 was still raging. There was no transport available for West Africa. The WEC leaders reasoned that if the women took a flight to Brazil there might be a flight from there to West Africa.

Helen and Adeline waited six long, boring, weeks in Natal, Brazil. Finally, Pan Am provided a flight to Liberia, the country next to Côte d'Ivoire. By faith the eager missionaries boarded.

On arrival in Liberia, they discovered there were no boats, buses, or planes for the rest of their journey. If they wanted to get to the place God called them, they would have to walk. It took three weeks to walk about 500 kilometres to the border. Tom was with them and very familiar with life in Africa. They hired Liberian boys to carry the baggage. The paths were well worn as this was the only way to and from the interior. They walked over swinging bridges attached to trees on either side of ravines. The final challenge was to cross a wide river—no bridge, no ferry, no canoes. The water was waist deep. The option was to walk across or be carried in a hammock held high above the heads of four men.

Several porters protested, "These women are too heavy." The men had to be persuaded. "I will go first," offered Helen, hopping into a hammock. The hammocks swung inches above the water. Adeline soon followed. It was great to arrive in Côte d'Ivoire, but more walking was required before a truck could take them to the nearest WEC mission station.

Since no communication was available their arrival was totally unexpected, but a small room was found where they could sleep. In the days ahead they settled into learning the culture and language of their adopted land. God had made a way.

I Surrender All

Beth Allinger in India, 1945

Beth Allinger heard God's call to join a new advance to the *closed lands* of Central Asia. Although she was accepted into WEC in 1942, she couldn't leave for India until 1945 because of the war. Finally, she linked up with WEC missionaries leaving New York on a Portuguese ship headed for India. It took four months to arrive in Goa where they boarded a train for the ten-hour trip to Bombay to make connections for North India. The train didn't get far when thieves climbed aboard and robbed everyone. The thieves then set fire to the train.

Even though all their precious belongings for life and ministry went up in smoke, the brave team did not turn back. They journeyed on to their destination, Darjeeling, over 2,000 kilometres away. The following year Beth joined coworker Elaine and moved to Assam where Beth served for 32 years and saw many souls turn to Christ.

IV

Missionary Life

And we know that in all things God works for the good of those who love him, who have been called according to his purpose.
Romans 8:28

Easy is not a word used to describe the life of a missionary. There are rewards, but material comfort is often not among them. Missionaries are faced with language and cultural barriers, confusing bureaucracy, intense heat, and/or local uprisings. Compound that with opposition from the powers of darkness and stronghold thinking and you wonder why more missionaries don't just give up.
But, God: He instills hope. He highlights his promises. He provides the miraculous. There is healing. There is salvation. Eyes and hearts are opened and it is all worth it.

A Year of Mishaps and Miracles

Beryl Shannon in Zaire, 1983

"So, this is what it's like to go to Heaven," I thought to myself as the train crashed into our Land Rover, smashing the door beside me.

The Land Rover didn't have a starter motor. My Scottish colleague Margaret White had sent the faulty part to the U.K. to get a replacement. A little thing like that couldn't stop us from driving the 70 kilometres north to Isiro to pick up medical supplies and other items from the shops. We simply gave the vehicle a push start at the beginning of each trip.

That day we collected the supplies and at noon had lunch with our American friends, two nurses who lived in Isiro, and now we were headed out of town to visit our fellow WEC missionaries at Gamba. Train tracks ran parallel to the road for several blocks before switching across the road to the other side. We could clearly see the train, two engines hooked back-to-back, but Margaret, the driver, assumed the train was going the opposite direction. Until we got to the crossover!

I screamed. At that, Margaret stalled the Land Rover. I leaned across the seat; sure I was going to Heaven. Margaret quickly turned the key and the vehicle started! She backed up so we were sitting at an angle on the track, which likely saved our lives because the train pushed us off the tracks rather than knocking us over.

At the side of the track where the train had pushed us, Margaret turned the key in the ignition once again, but nothing happened—as to be expected without a starter motor. Praise God for miracles. Neither of us was badly hurt, just minor bruising and a wound on my ankle. That night, back at our friends' apartment, God gave me Psalms 116 and 118. Such a blessing they were as I meditated on these words, *"For You have delivered my soul from death, my eyes from tears and my feet from falling. I will walk before the LORD in the land of the living."* Psalm 116:8,9.

* * *

Later that same year, I flew by MAF (Mission Aviation Fellowship) down to Mulita, our mission station in the south, to stay with Ida Grainger, whose husband had recently passed on. On a sunny Sunday morning, we were about to leave for church, when we heard a great commotion outside. Ida went to the door and found a man standing on our doorstep, shouting, "There's a rabid dog on the loose; watch out for him." We needed to be careful.

At that moment, I heard a low growl inside the house. I looked around. Sure enough, a little dog was quivering beneath the book shelf. Ida took up the broom to encourage him to go outside. Instead, he came straight for me and bit my leg. Ida quickly got me into her Land Rover to take me to Punia, two hours away. While we were getting ready to leave, God spoke to me. He told me, *"This is not unto death."*

When we arrived at the hospital, we found that they had just received a shipment of rabies medicine the day previous—a miracle. They had been without it for nearly a year. I was able to get the necessary injection. The following day, MAF picked me up from the grass airstrip at Mulita and flew me to Nebobongo Hospital where I continued with treatment for a few more weeks. It happened just as God had promised, I did not die. Praise God.

* * *

In 1983, snakes were a problem in Nebobongo. We had no screens on our windows, just shutters and wooden bars to keep thieves out, but they did nothing to keep snakes out of our homes. Hence, we lived with a watchful eye. Maud Kells, from North Ireland, and I shared a house, so at least we were not alone in our vigilance. One time Maud was bitten by a venomous snake while rushing to get medicine for a sick patient. She shook it off, just as Paul did, and kept on going. No harm done.

Not so long after that as I was reading in bed as was my habit, I saw a flicker of movement on my bed: a baby black mamba, about three feet long (adults are often nearly ten feet long) had crawled through my window. Of course I screamed, "Nyoka, nyoka!"

Maud ran to call Daudi, our house help, while I stayed by to keep my eye on the snake. If it hid itself somewhere in my room, we would have had to evacuate the house until it was found and dealt with. Daudi appeared with his machete and dispatched the mamba, much to our relief and gratitude. The black mamba is considered to be Africa's deadliest snake. Had I not still been reading with my light on, I would not have seen the snake. Once again, God proved himself faithful in miraculously taking care of me.

* * *

Then just before Christmas 1983, I went to Isiro for a few days before flying to Itendey, to spend Christmas with the Brethren missionaries. I well remember staying those few days with the American nurses in town. Sometimes they had electricity in their home, and sometimes not. This day, not, so I was cooking a pot of beans on a kerosene burner on the cupboard in their tiny kitchen. As I chatted with my friends, I didn't realize the pot was gradually moving closer and closer to the edge of the cupboard. I jumped back when the burner slid off and crashed onto the floor. Immediately, the kerosene caught fire and flames shot high to the ceiling. The whole kitchen was flammable with cookbooks on a shelf below the cupboard, wooden cupboards, wooden ceiling and very thin curtains on the window. It could so easily have all caught fire—the whole building, including the printing press downstairs on the main floor. Yet, nothing burned, except the kerosene. One of the girls managed to push the burner out the door and down the outside stairs with a broom. Smoke and flames were everywhere. But nothing burned. A miracle.

* * *

These stories could have ended in death, except for God's miraculous interventions. Yet, the greatest miracle of all was that many people came to know Jesus in Zaire. They had walked the path of death long enough, now Jesus gave them the miracle of everlasting life.

Pioneering Medical Work

Marion Congo in Liberia, 1940's

On March 8, 1940, Kay Tullis and I sailed from New York aboard a Barber Line freighter. Three weeks later we anchored with the city of Monrovia in view. We disembarked by means of a rope ladder and were rowed in a surf boat to the wharf.

There was no one to meet us because the cablegram telling of our arrival had been delayed. Fellow passengers, who were with the America Bank, graciously gave us hospitality until Mr. Davey came for us.

We travelled down the coast in a surf boat. In the evening an equinoctial storm overtook us. Waves 40 feet high challenged our safety and progress. The sailors hauled down the sail. Everyone was drastically seasick. But the storm subsided in a few hours. Night passed and the sun came out to dry and warm us. By noon we found ourselves at Lower Buchanan. This time, strong men carried us on their shoulders to the shore.

Language study was our first assignment, but within a couple of weeks I began caring for local people who needed medical help. Before the end of May, a crude temporary dispensary was arranged. As more people heard of the doctor woman, it became necessary to set regular dispensary hours. Many came with ulcers, malarial fever, worms and secondary symptoms of yaws. As soon as I obtained intravenous injections, there was a constant stream of patients with primary yaws. How grateful they were when the yellow-button lesions healed within three weeks. It was a great joy to help in this way. A message telling the good news of salvation was given before the medicines were dispensed, therefore, many found the Lord through the medical work.

Mrs. Carol Davey, the field leader's wife was my first patient with malarial fever. A month later Kay Tullis came down with it (and again the following month) so I was also nursing the missionary staff as well as participating in a full program of village evangelism.

About a year later I broke out with primary lesions caused by yaws. My feet were so painful I spent time in bed. The Lord illumined James chapter five to my understanding. At my request, Percy Clubine and Bill Freeman (enroute to the Ivory Coast) anointed me and prayed for healing.

What a reassuring experience to see this condition cleared up and have a speedy return to health and vitality.

***Travail, Triumph, Jubilee**, (1989) edited by Hellen J. Kuleskey, pages 26-7*

Establishing a School is a Priority

Marion Congo in Liberia, 1940's

After our arrival in Gaypeter in early 1940, my travelling companion, Kay Tullis at once began an elementary school. A well-qualified and experienced teacher, she set up a carefully outlined curriculum. The children and young people were quick to recognize her ability. How they respected and loved her.

A larger, temporary school was erected in July— a mud and stick building with a thatch roof. With a homemade desk for each pupil, it was then practical to leave books and supplies where they were used each day.

Since Kay was the only teacher on the station, I was her substitute when she was away or was ill.

In February 1942, Herb Congo and Tom Jackson, two Canadians who had arrived in early 1941, worked on the permanent brick school building as well as a brick dormitory for the school boys. Those were very heavy work days for all of us, but we were rewarded by the sight of the eager young faces of those who had come to learn. We soon had 20 students and were expecting quite a few more.

Making clothes for the youngsters was quite a problem. We didn't know what we would use to make trousers for some of the boys, as cloth was quite expensive during the war and what we were able to get was none too durable. We ended up ripping Kay Tullis' old winter coat. The woolen cloth made three pair of short trousers, and the flannelette inner lining made several pair of briefer shorts suitable for work. Only the rayon lining remained. God surely does supply our needs one way or another.

Travail, Triumph, Jubilee, *(1989) edited by Hellen J. Kuleskey, page 33.*

Pioneering

Helen Krueger and Adeline Wilke in Côte d'Ivoire, 1944-1996

Before going to Ivory Coast in Africa, I, Helen, had the idea that once I brought the people the good news of Jesus, they would immediately embrace Christianity. One missionary hymn says the heathen are crying out, "How long, how long must we wait?" It was quite a disappointment when we found many were not interested in hearing and accepting God's word. Once Adeline came across an old Gouro woman with leprosy, huddled up by a fire in her dim hut. Her foot and hand were partly eaten away. Flies swarmed around her open sores. Our hearts went out in compassion and we desired to tell her about God's love. We told her about how God so loved the world that he sent the Saviour, that she might be cleansed and be ready to go to God's village. She responded by saying she had followed the devil all her life and that she loved the devil and wanted to go live with him.

She said God had never done anything for her. Hearing her say, "Go away and leave me alone," was devastating. At times like these, when the devil's hold on lives is challenged, the unseen spiritual battle with the forces of darkness can almost be felt physically. One would be afraid if one did not know that Satan is a defeated foe.

How I longed that many would come to know God. Sometimes I felt we were accomplishing so little as we went about having meetings. People were so bound with their superstitions and were so slow to believe. God, however, asks only that we be faithful and obedient, and leave the rest to Him. We believed that soon more would turn to Him. It was encouraging that many of the younger generation seemed to be listening attentively.

Once we arrived in a village just as a chief was about to judge a woman who had committed adultery. Those in attendance had mixed up a poison drink, and were about to force her to drink it. They believed that if she was innocent, it would not kill her, but if she was guilty, she would die. This practice was strictly forbidden by the French, so because we were there, they were afraid to carry it out. The woman was spared. We never knew if they proceeded after we left.

In December of 1951 Adeline and I were sleeping in our mission house in Oumé. As always, we slept with our windows open for air, with mosquito netting around our twin beds. There were no bars on the windows and Adeline and I were never afraid. Until one night at 4 a.m. I heard Adeline suddenly scream that someone was trying to kill her. Her bed was nearest to the window. I pulled my flashlight from under the pillow in time to see a man with a club climbing out. I was unable to see who it was.

Adeline's mosquito net had been torn from its frame and she felt her arm was broken. We got into our car and headed for the home of our Christian doctor friend. As we were driving down the hill, we heard footsteps on the gravel. Then a rock flew in through the passenger window and grazed Adeline.

When we arrived at the doctor's, he found that her arm was not broken but needed a sling. He advised us to wait at his house until daybreak when his wife accompanied us back to the mission house.

Upon returning, we entered the bedroom, where Adeline asked me to tie her head scarf. While tying, I had my back to the door. Suddenly a man rushed in with a club and smacked me on the head. I nearly fainted. Adeline recognized the man, as he scrambled out. We were dismayed to find out who had attacked us. He was one of our Christians who was in the last stages of sleeping sickness. During the first stages of the disease people do not even know that they have the disease, but later on they develop sleeping spells. In the final stages, people become violent, and often try to kill the people they love the most. We had never had any problem with this man who attended church faithfully. Adeline ran after him to take his club. He, in turn, picked up a piece of metal guttering and struck her across the face, cutting her ear. Then he disappeared into the bush. We returned to the doctor's home. They told us to get our camp beds. We could sleep in their living room.

Even though the man was sent to an institution 60 kilometres away, we realized we could not return to the mission house as the shock had so upset our nerves that we could not sleep and were jumping at every noise. We were advised to go to the coast to take a short holiday at the ocean. The best thing for us was to get into a new area and try to forget the past.

We knew God had called us to Mankono, a completely unreached area.

The first thing to do was to establish a mission station. A sympathetic government official helped persuade some village chiefs to grant us a parcel of ground. We cleared the bush and started making mud bricks for our mud huts. With the help of local Africans and under the supervision of our mission director, the first building went up. As we built, we also tried to reach out to the nearby villages with the gospel.

Not many accepted the gospel. We had some converts amongst the Muslims, but it was handpicked fruit. I would like to tell you about Lakika. Lakika was a Muslim lad, about fourteen years old, going to a government school. One day, while I was working in our flower garden on our mission station, I looked up, and here was this lad asking, "Mademoiselle, can you show me how I might become a Christian?"

I replied, "Why yes, come into the house. Why do you want to become a Christian?"

"I got the loan of a Bible from one of your Christians, and I read, and I read, and I read, and I saw that Jesus Christ is the Son of God."

"You are Muslim, are you not?"

"Yes."

"Do you know what this is going to cost you?"

"Yes, I know. My Father is a very strong Muslim. He is a teacher of the Koran and has made the pilgrimage to Mecca. I know I must be obedient to my parents, but in this one thing, I must be obedient to God."

I then proceeded to give him the gospel from the beginning to the end. He listened very carefully. When I finished, I said to him, "Did you understand?"

"I understood very well."

"When do you want to become a Christian?"

"I want to become a Christian right now; that is why I have come."

We knelt on the floor and Lakika prayed a prayer that the Father in heaven heard and the angels in heaven rejoiced to hear—the sinner's prayer. When he finished, I prayed for him and gave him several verses to assure him of his salvation. I also gave him a New Testament and encouraged him to read it and to come each day for a Bible study, which he did. One day, when he found the passage almost immediately, I said, "Lakika, how did you find that so quickly?"

He said, "I have been reading this, and it is all so precious."

We still had to build an actual mission house. We had looked at the layout of other mission houses, but nothing seemed suitable for our needs. We would have to have a living room big enough for our church services, because Muslims will not come into a church, but they will come to a house.

One night in 1952, I dreamt that Helen and I were standing in our mission compound looking at the perfect mission house for our needs and said, "Isn't that a beautiful home." In the morning, I didn't say anything to Helen but in the afternoon during rest time, I drew the plan of the house I had seen in the dream. It was in the form of a T. When I showed Helen the plan, she asked where I got the plan, and so I told her. About a week later, I received a letter from my father and as I began to read, tears came to my eyes. Helen asked if someone had died in my family and I said, "No, but listen to this...." My father had written, "Last night, while I was on my knees praying, the Lord spoke to me and said, 'Send this money out to your daughter.' I don't know what the need is, but there must be a need." He had sent $1,000.

About two weeks later, Helen received a letter from her brother, a farmer and a Christian, and he said the Lord had spoken to him in the spring of the year to put aside a parcel of land for the Lord, to sow the seed and harvest it for him. He did and when it was harvested, he asked the Lord what he should do with the money and the Lord told him to send it out to his sister. The amount came to $1,000.

We contacted our field leader and told him to send Stan the builder. We had the plan and $2,000. It was not the full amount needed, but we knew we could trust in the Lord for all of it. Stan could take on as many workmen as needed. Stan said he would like to make the house according to the plan, but with two improvements and we agreed. It took six months to build the house.

Never did we stop the construction for lack of funds. When the building was dedicated to the Lord, there was not one cent of debt against it. This, in itself, was a miracle.

Work among the Senoufo: There were Senoufo villages about 100 kilometres north of Mankono. These are hardworking people. They work on their farms from early morning until dark.

Among the Senoufos, often it is the wife who accepts the gospel first. The husbands can be very cruel, trying their best to get their wives to return to paganism. They make their believing wives work harder in the fields, and refuse to buy them clothes.

After trying in vain to get his wife to turn away from Christ, one man decided to take another wife. This was his effort to get his first wife to turn back to the fetish. She did not waver and instead of being jealous, she witnessed to the second wife, leading her to become a believer. They both then attended church. Now the man had two Christian wives and was very angry.

At this point, he became very sick and thought he was going to die. All his fetish medicine and sacrifices were not working. In desperation, he called the Christian men to come and pray for him. He recovered and became a believer, attending church and sitting in the front bench. He would clap and sing with the others. As pagans, these people are 100 percent for the devil but when they are truly converted, they became 100 percent for the Lord, trying to win others so they also would find peace and joy.

Once our Bible School had trained some nationals, we recruited two to help us evangelize. Later on, pastors that were fully trained were available and we had Pastor Samuel sent to us. The Lord used him in amazing ways. Pastor

Samuel prayed for the sick, lame and blind and many were healed.

Bamoussa, a Muslim, had been blind for eight years and was led about by a boy holding a stick for him to grasp. His family tried every native medicine, fetish medicine and drug store medicine with no results. When he heard about Pastor Samuel, he agreed that someone accompany him to see Pastor Samuel, but said he would never become a Christian even if he were healed. After three days of hearing the testimony of many who were healed, he got up one morning and found his eyes were opened and he could see. He was overwhelmed with joy and shouted the news to others. He had been prayed for in Jesus' name and declared that since Jesus had opened his eyes, he would no longer be a Muslim and wanted to become a Christian.

He talked to Pastor Samuel and said he wanted to know what was written in the Bible, but he had never gone to school and was not able to read. He asked the pastor to pray for him that God would open his intelligence and cause him to read right away. Pastor Samuel asked if he believed Jesus could do it and he said, "Didn't he open my eyes? Yes, I know he can open my intelligence to read." The pastor prayed and then handed him a New Testament, which he opened and started to read. What a miracle! He grew spiritually and then went to the Baptist Bible School at Korhogo for four years and became a full-time pastor. God also gave him a wonderful and talented wife.

Once Bamoussa was with me on a trek to a Muslim village where there were no Christians. He usually preached first for half an hour and then I took over. As he preached, he saw as it were, a vision of all the people of the town headed towards the fires of hell and he was overwhelmed with compassion. Right in front of the crowd, he burst into tears and could not continue. I took over and explained how the reality of an eternal hell was a real truth and they needed to accept Christ as he is the only way to heaven. Pastor Bamoussa continues to minister to Muslims at Booko and people really listen.

In 1958 Adeline and I left new missionaries to carry on at Mankono and headed for the unreached area of Touba, a Muslim area. On arrival, we went to visit the paramount chief, to tell him who we were and why we had come. He listened and wanted us to come back in the evening to talk. He said his wife could cook a meal of rice and chicken. We prayed that God would help us present our message to him and that he would allow us to come and evangelize in all the more than 250 villages.

After the meal, the chief asked us to explain our religion. We started with Adam and Eve, (a common ground as they believed the creation story and the fall of man), and then we went on to show how, as sinners, we need a Saviour. Our good works cannot take away our sin. We told him how God sent Jesus to be our Saviour and we know if Christ forgives us, we will go to heaven. Then he told us about his religion. He proceeded to tell us that Muslims hope that by their prayers, good deeds and fasting, Allah will allow them to go to heaven. Then he said something that impressed me. He said, "You Christians have a know-so religion while Muslims have a hope-so religion." Muslims have no assurance of heaven because they have no Saviour to forgive their sins. Then he told us that we could stay in Touba and visit all the villages and preach. What an open door.

In all, we drove five different vehicles, which the Lord supplied through the gifts from family and friends back in Canada. In all the 52 years, we never asked for money but just looked to God to supply and he moved upon hearts to give. Whether we needed a vehicle or house or a furlough, He always came through. Never once did we have to cancel a planned trek or necessary trip or conference for lack of gas.

Our 52 years with WEC have been wonderful. We have had such a good fellowship with each other and I thank God for every fellow worker. We have stood with each other in difficult times and shared when there were times of need. I had the privilege of teaching the Dioula language to about 20 new workers, one or two at a time, as they arrived on the field. At the same time, I initiated them in adapting to the culture, food and life in general. It was always exciting to see the progress and success when they could give their first message in a village.

In early 2000, after retirement, I went back to Côte d'Ivoire for a three-month visit. I visited all the places where I had worked those 52 years. I saw how much the churches had grown with African pastors and leaders. God showed me that my ministry there was finished and I now willingly close that chapter of my life. I have peace accepting God's will and am happy to remain in Canada. I can pray, encourage others to pray and encourage younger people to go. The doors are still open and the need for workers is great.

Chosen to Go *by Helen E. Krueger, excerpts from throughout the book.*

Feeling Like an Outcast

Ellen Gillman in Thailand, 1950

In September 1950, Paul Arnold a Presbyterian missionary attached to the McKean Leprosarium in Chiang Mai, came to our area as he was making a survey of leprosy in Thailand. Leprosy was a terrible scourge at that time and although we missionaries did have an answer to every leper's spiritual need, we had no cure for those disfigured by the dread disease.

Paul examined healthy looking children and adults as we WECers looked on. A blindfold was placed over each person's eyes and a piece of soft cotton was gently rubbed along areas of the back, shoulders, neck, ears and face, then moved down to the arms and legs. "Anaesthesia is one of the first symptoms," Paul explained. "That loss of sensation is what allows burns and sores to go untreated. A leper can step on a burning charcoal spark and not know that his foot is burning until he smells his burned flesh."

A blanket of dread settled over me. I had noticed areas of anaesthesia around my ankle bones for some time and had wondered what it was. I was no longer a smiling disinterested observer. I knew that I had often played with children who Paul said were infected with leprosy. I thought of the homes of lepers I had visited and of the many buses I had ridden on—there were hundreds of places I could have contracted the disease.

"I have an area of anaesthesia," I said as calmly as I could. Everyone looked at me in startled horror. I was put through the blindfold test and beyond doubt, I had the symptoms of leprosy.

A sentence of death hung over me. I was told to no longer have any physical contact with any healthy person, not even with Rosemary, my fellow worker. I needed to keep my dishes separate from hers. Then I remembered how often I had played with the Overgaard children. I was 'Aunty Ellen' and they often sat on my lap. I felt like an outcast. I didn't dare touch them nor touch their toys. That long, lonely bus ride to the Leprosarium was one I will never forget. I didn't look like a leper and my fellow passengers were not afraid of me, but this was the first time I refused helping hands offering to assist me. I felt the taste of being an outcast. A leper! A cloud of darkness and fear settled upon me.

Three days of intense testing followed. Tests much more intensive than that simple blindfold test were performed. Then a joyful announcement was made, "Ellen, you are not a leper. The anaesthesia on your ankles is the result of many hours of sitting on the bamboo matting. The nerve endings on your ankles have been destroyed, but you do not have leprosy.

It was my brush with leprosy that led our WEC Thailand team to become involved with the treatment of leprosy. Understanding the feeling of being an outcast and being able to sympathize with them, helped me greatly in my years of ministry in Thailand.

The Opienge Revival

Hulda Brown in Congo, 1953

What we called the Opienge revival, started as a result of what the wife of one of our church elders had to say in a meeting one Sunday. She said, "When we Africans want to light a fire in the mornings, what is the first thing we do? Is it not that we take a broom and sweep away the ashes from the fireplace where yesterday's fire went out? We then place the wood in order, and then we go and get a live coal from someone else's fire to light our own fire. Soon it burns brightly. But if we don't clean the ashes away the fire is not very good."

Then she made the application saying, "We Christians need to clean the ashes out of our hearts, and then the fire of God will burn brightly!"

Immediately there was a moving of God's spirit in our midst, and that was the beginning of the revival at Opienge in 1953. Church leaders were the first to confess their sins, and others followed. Meetings went on for hours at a time as folks got right with God. Then there was great rejoicing. At times the whole congregation would stand to their feet with hands raised towards heaven. They would sing and praise the Lord Jesus for his precious blood. These revival meetings continued for several months. My husband and I were happy to be there at this time and to be part of this wonderful visitation of God.

River of Memories *(2001) by Hulda Brown, pages 66–7.*

God's Grace, Love and Power Demonstrated

Hellen Kuleskey in Liberia, 1955-1963

My seven years in Liberia as a member of Liberia Inland Mission (a WEC organization) were spent primarily in the classrooms, except for weekend treks to surrounding villages. My outstanding memories, however, are not centred in school activities or preaching, but rather in what I experienced of God's grace and love through my Liberian brothers and sisters in Christ.

I recall one of my first semi-annual church conferences held on Bahn station. One believer after another rose to testify of God's faithfulness in the activities of everyday life. One lady, an only believer in a distant village, told us how she was challenged to pray for a seriously ill neighbour. All traditional remedies had proved futile and the patient was on the verge of death. In desperation, the townsfolk came to the sister and said, "You are a Christian. Here, pray for this woman that she not die." The prayer of faith in the name of Jesus restored the ill person. My heart flooded with praise to the God that heals the sick as he promised in his word through the Apostle James and others. However, what amazed me was this babe in Christ. The extent of her knowledge of the things of God was limited to a few songs which she taught to the village children during her morning prayers. She was untrained in the word and unable to read it for herself. But the Holy Spirit within her knew the word perfectly and glorified Jesus through her faith.

At the same conference, a brother who was a hunter stood to testify how God delivered him during a hunting expedition undertaken at night. The lamp he wore on his forehead first flickered and then ceased to function altogether in spite of the shaking he gave it. Panic-stricken at being caught in the forest in the blackness of the night, he cried to the Lord to save him. Suddenly an amazing number of fireflies appeared enabling him to sufficiently see the path home. As he walked, however, the thought occurred to him that he had never seen anything like this before and he began to fear for a different reason. Then God spoke to his heart, "First you pray and when I answer, then you are afraid." These words assured the hunter that this strange phenomenon was his heavenly father's intervention to a cry of faith.

One incident demonstrating the grace of love stands out in my memory to continually bless me. One weekend I walked to a village some fifteen miles away. Not used to traversing such long distances on foot, I was totally exhausted. I wondered if I could do more than lay my weary body down and recuperate for the equally long distance back. But the exciting welcome that awaited our party at our destination revived my sagging spirits. One by one the village women came to greet me and present me with a gift—a traditional token of their welcome. And one true servant of Christ obeyed the prompting of the Lord and in the spirit of Jesus—who girded himself with a towel and washed the disciples' feet—stooped down and lovingly dusted off the sneakers on my burning feet. It was as though Jesus himself stooped to caress one of his weary children.

Not only does God reveal his grace to us, he also reveals his power. This he did during a terrifying electrical storm one fierce rainy season. It was suppertime and we had barely started eating when someone flung open the kitchen door and stumbled in. The breathless young man announced that the Bible school campus was hit by lightning and that one of the student wives, Martha, had been struck. He dashed back into the storm to call the town Christians for prayer.

We found Martha unconscious. "Throw her on the ground and let the fire come out of her," someone shouted, but medical know-how prevailed and we treated Martha for shock. I scrounged for warm blankets and hot water bottles, dashing back and forth in the bone-chilling rain before I joined the prayer group. That is where the real battle for Martha's life was waged.

"Lord, you know if this woman dies, the heathen will say that our God is not any stronger than their gods," our director, Percy Clubine, prayed in a concerned, tired voice. It seems I heard no more until Martha sat up an hour and a half later and said, "I am thirsty." A final burst of joy and praise to God the healer came some months later when Martha delivered the baby she was then carrying. The precious little one was totally normal!

I later asked Donald, the jubilant husband and father, for an account of this deliverance for publication in the fledgling Youth paper I was then duplicating and distributing within the republic. Donald Wuanti wrote the following: "For 25 years we have heard how Jesus healed the sick and raised the dead and now we have seen it."

The years in Liberia (1955-1963) initiated my full-time service as a missionary. They are indelibly etched in my mind, no doubt because God's grace, love and power became more real to me through my interaction with his children in Liberia.

***Travail, Triumph, Jubilee**, (1989) edited by Hellen J. Kuleskey, pages 36-8.*

Handling a Missionary Medical Career and Motherhood

Nancy Wood, M.D. in Zaire, Liberia and Canada, 1978 - 1988

One of the challenges that faces many women called to serve the Lord in missions is the apparent conflict between a missionary career and motherhood. So many people have yet to hear the gospel; so many new believers need to be discipled; so many neighbours need help with literacy and health problems. How is it possible to divide one's time between these needs and the needs of growing children? I believe God has an answer to that question for each woman who asks it. The way he leads in sorting out priorities will bring glory to his name and leave no regrets for the one who is obedient.

God led me into a marriage and to a career in missionary medicine. When our first child was born, what were God's priorities for me? I faced this question after four years of fulfilling work at *Centre Medical Evangélique* in Nyankunde, Zaire. Would I ask a local woman, perhaps a grandmother in her own right, to be available to babysit from six-thirty in the morning to five at night while I worked in the hospital and the nursing school? Or would I relinquish my professional responsibilities and be a mom at home? If I were to leave hospital medicine at this point, would it ever be possible to catch up and get back in again? Some would say unlikely, others impossible.

I had already worked through the question of cooking and cleaning. In Zaire where food preparation and cooking are an all-day occupation, it obviously made sense for me to pay someone to be in the kitchen and allow me to do my doctoring. Similarly, washing clothes by hand and cleaning a house could be assigned to someone else. But what about mothering?

In my hospital work I had focused particularly on sick children. I realized that many more babies would have died early had it not been that almost all mothers faithfully breast-fed their children. I spent many hours in the classroom, at the bedside and in the children's clinics affirming the mothers in their role and encouraging them to continue nursing their babies as long as possible. How many times had I said that the use of a baby bottle is equivalent to a death certificate? Could I now plan to do anything other than I had been preaching? Practically speaking, I probably could have worked full time and returned home briefly every three to four hours to continue breast-feeding, but the deep conviction of my heart was that for a period of time I was to be first of all a mother.

The Bible verse that influenced me most was Proverbs 22:6: *"Train a child in the way he should go and when he is old, he will not turn from it."* A simple interpretation of this verse implies that some action is to take place and that a child is not born with nor does he spontaneously develop all the ideal traits of character and right desires. Clearly someone has to take the responsibility for guiding, directing, teaching and training. My husband affirmed my role as mother as did our reading of James Dobson's book, *Dare to Discipline*.

Jérémie's arrival brought lots of joy and Grandma came from Canada to lend a hand and supply encouragement for a month. Once basic routines were established there was time to consider fitting in a few career responsibilities. Initially I agreed to teach nutrition one hour per day in the nursing school while Jérémie had his morning nap. He was a little man of great predictability and the system worked well. The five-minute walk from home to the school was convenience at its best.

A few months later, the medical director suggested that I be responsible for the medical care of the 50 missionaries and their children at Nyankunde. They were often so busy with their work that they were unable to be seen by a doctor in regular office hours, and he certainly did not want them to be neglected. Thus began a small family practice based mostly on house calls. In the daytime Jérémie enjoyed the outings in his stroller. A visit by car in the evenings when my husband Philip was home was another option.

On home leave in Canada, Timothy joined the family, and after six months in Switzerland at Emmaus Bible Institute we returned to Zaire. Once we were settled in our new house with a responsible teenager in the kitchen and a grandma doing the housekeeping, some teaching and house calls were once again part of my program. The opportunity also came to tutor some fourth-year nursing students one evening per week. They were expected to do a small individual research project during their final year and to write a brief paper about their findings. The projects needed careful supervision which I enjoyed giving weekly throughout their entire final year. That session was conveniently arranged after the children were in bed.

Keeping up-to-date medically usually involves some refresher courses for doctors. The Christian Medical & Dental Society of the USA and the University of Louisville in Kentucky together organized ten-day courses for missionary doctors. What a refreshing break to attend these sessions in Kenya. During each course a Bible school program was provided for the children. I believe God's order for me was to make mothering my first priority. Then in His faithfulness God showed me ways, while my children were small, to use my professional skills.

In 1988 when we moved to Liberia and anticipated our sons attending ELWA (Eternal Love Winning Africa) Academy, I offered to work at ELWA Hospital during the hours the boys were in school. Philip started work in the hospital shortly after we arrived. According to the schedule he brought home, on my first morning at work I was assigned to the emergency room after ward rounds, and working in the obstetrics clinic on Tuesdays. After ten years away from hospital work, how was I going to cope with these challenges? I lay awake at night scared stiff and feeling totally inadequate. During our furlough in Toronto, I had taken some Saturday courses to get up-to-date, but none of them had included patients or emergencies. This time the schedule seemed like an impossible hurdle even for God.

On the first day of school, we sent the boys on their way to classes to begin at seven-thirty in the morning and Philip and I went to the hospital. We started with prayers in the chapel. By this time the Lord might have been tired of hearing the same prayer from me: "Lord, please help me make no mistakes and deal with my inadequacies." During ward rounds I was relieved to find that not much was required of me. A congenial atmosphere prevailed in which the management of the many seriously ill patients was discussed by all the doctors, and the dreaded hurdle became a good learning experience. My heart shouted, "Thank you, Lord."

Later, my supervising doctor said not much would be happening in the emergency room on Monday morning. He suggested that I go with him to the outpatients' department and begin learning the ropes there. What a blessing! I wasn't going to be thrown in at the deep end after all. About a week later a new doctor joined the staff. He had just graduated in internal medicine with honours from the Yale School of Medicine at Yale University. He would be up-to-date on everything! What would he think of an older female doctor who was feeling rusty? It didn't take long to discover that he was a humble young man who had a tremendous amount of knowledge stored away in an orderly fashion and was only too willing to answer any questions and teach the listener.

I should have known that God would also show his faithfulness in helping me in the obstetrics clinic. The boss had me work along with him for a couple of months, examining the women with complications. We had the advantage of our own ultrasound machine, so I learned that technique too. How I thanked the Lord for colleagues who were patient teachers.

When it came to school holidays, I felt that my place was really at home. On most days my colleagues were willing to cover for me, but help was needed on Wednesday mornings in the outpatient clinic. God had an answer for that one too. My prayer partner's nursing skills were needed in the obstetrical clinic on Tuesdays. So, while she worked, her three children came to my house, and while I worked my two went to her house. Jérémie still has on his wall the string art picture that my friend helped him create. Thank you, Lord, for beautiful friendships.

The civil war in Liberia cut our anticipated years of service there to two.

God worked through individuals and circumstances to show us that he would have us work in WEC Canada in Hamilton. Philip and I both felt it was right for me to remain in medical work to better serve WEC missionaries and to be fully up-to-date for the time when the Lord might call us back to Africa. But considering my role and responsibilities in the large house that serves as WEC Canada's headquarters, it became obvious that I would be able to do medical work only on Mondays.

Here was another challenge for the Lord. How would a missionary doctor find a medical job in Canada with just the right hours and in a very competitive job market? In the first few months as we adjusted to life in Canada in a new city, I made a few inquiries about work, but they came to nothing. I called the medical faculty of McMaster University to ask about their individualized courses for doctors, but the director advised that all I needed was to work along with an experienced family doctor. But who? I felt certain God had something for me beginning that January, but what?

At Christmas a young doctor who had become a Christian during his elective at Nyankunde came, with his wife, to visit us. They asked about us doing medical work, and I explained that I felt it was right for me to do some and shared the conditions. They had the answer. The wife's mom, a Christian lady in private family practice in Hamilton, was finding her load a little heavy and was looking for help. She was only too willing to accept me without references, without a written contract and on my conditions because I had been part of the team that helped her son-in-law come to know Jesus.

It is more than five years since I began my job with a boss who is sympathetic to missions and willingly gives me time off for WEC business travel, conferences, short-term mission stints and holidays. What a blessing. God did it again.

When we are tempted to feel torn apart in the face of an impossible decision, God has an answer. He wants us to seek his priorities and be in tune with the work he is doing. When we submit to his leading, he can do abundantly more than we are able to ask or imagine (Ephesians 3:20).

The Adventure of Working with God *edited by Marjorie McDermid, pages 9-15.*

Missionary Boy

Hulda Brown in Congo, 1964

One evening our six-year-old son, David, and his father went for a walk. In this part of Africa close to the equator, there is no twilight. Darkness falls suddenly around 6:30 p.m. every night, no matter whether it is rainy or dry season. Thus, in gathering darkness, they set off on their walk and stopped to chat when they came to the pastor's house.

While my husband chatted, David was drawn to a young man sitting at a fire next door. Moses was sitting outside his house staring into the fire and David quietly sat down beside him. Together they watched the intricate flames dancing about. Moses was in deep thought and didn't talk. As the flames died down with only glowing embers remaining, David asked him why he was so sad. David had not yet received his answer when his father called to say, "We have to go now." They walked back to our house and David was soon tucked away in his bed and fast asleep.

All was quiet in the house, when we heard a faint knock at the door. My husband went to answer and who was there, but Moses. When asked what we could do for him, he said, "When David asked me tonight why I was so sad, I began to think about it. I wondered why I was sad?" Then Moses proceeded to say that perhaps it was because he did not have Jesus in his heart, and that he wanted to ask him in. That was a happy day for Moses as he opened his heart to the Saviour. .... **Children can be missionaries too**!

River of Memories *(2001) by Hulda Brown, pages 85-6.*

Divine Protection

Margie Knapp in The Gambia, 1981

T*he angel of the Lord encamps around those who fear him, and rescues them. Psalm 34:7*

It was July 1981. I had been a missionary in The Gambia for almost two years. I lived at the WEC mission headquarters and clinic located near the capital city, Banjul. The clinic treated 300 to 400 patients a day.

A coup d'etat was attempted by a Marxist-Leninist group from Libya—mostly young Gambians trained in Libya and sent back to stage the coup. There was no army in The Gambia, only a national field force. Neighbouring Senegal sent their army to put down the coup. We missionaries and staff, along with the whole population, were in lockdown, existing on rations. On the seventh day at one o'clock in the afternoon, as our team was gathered for prayer, the army opened fire on our compound suspecting that there were rebels hiding within. In seconds, the 12 of us were on the floor, covered with large cushions. Every window in the mission house was shattered, except for the ones in the large sitting room we were in. The deafening sound of tank fire lasted about 30 minutes.

We remained on the floor for a while praying, singing and reading scripture. Not one of us was hurt. Our large supply of medicines and food was untouched. We thanked God because in other places, people were terrorized and robbed. About 1,000 lost their lives.

Picnicking in the Hills

Elsie Swan (age 10) in Chad 2023

One of my favourite things to do is to go for a picnic in the hills. I make breakfast the night before and then with my brothers and sisters, mom and dad we go by rickshaw to the hills around six o'clock in the morning. We carry a bag with boiled eggs, cinnamon buns, apples, cinnamon cake and four bottles of water at least. We drive about half an hour on very bumpy roads toward the two mountains or high hills just outside of the city. We go past the animal market where we sometimes see goats, or sheep or camels and then we start to climb up the mountain.

When we find a good place, we put a blanket on the ground to keep us from getting poked by thorns and then we sit down to a nice breakfast. We keep going and running on the hills after that until it's too hot and we are almost out of water. Then we start back towards our house. We walk to the road and wait for a rickshaw to come. We drive home, unpack and then we rest the rest of the day.

50 And Rising

Peter in Türkiye, 1998

"It's been three months. Write a prayer letter!" she said before leaving for the beach with the kids. The thermometer rose to 50 Celsius and still the red fluid kept rising. The world was an overheated sauna.

We filled the bathtub and slipped into it when conditions became unbearable—air conditioning was for the rich. It had not rained since spring. Wildfires broke out nearby. Our daughter, Rita suffered from recurring bouts of vomiting that summer and her budgie hadn't the oomph to raise its head above its shoulders. Neither did I. Stupefied and stripped to the waist, I nodded over my desk. Even after midnight it remained in the upper thirties. And the humidity! Locals call Adana Turkey's armpit for a reason.

Had three months passed since our last circular? What was there to report? We were still there, which we hoped was good news for the Kurds. We'd had a holiday in Northern Cyprus, and that had been good for us. I'd led two small church groups, one from Belgium and one from Canada, around the country, hoping they would carry a vision for the Middle East back to their home churches. Our team had grown to seven, including the single guy who lived with us that summer. We were grateful for unity and mutual support as we attempted to set goals, trying to determine what ministries they could engage in now that they were coming to grips with the language and the culture. How does one reach the Kurds without getting deported? That was the question.

What else? We'd survived an earthquake. Some people were killed, many more wounded. Most of Adana's buildings were damaged, many beyond repair. Our apartment too sported impressive cracks. Aftershocks continued for weeks. That and the intense heat encouraged many to flee for the mountains or the sea, leaving the city a ghost town. Death was on everyone's mind, and it was easy to speak of eternity with those who remained.

After the earthquake Anna had escorted Owen and Rita and four other kids to a children's camp in Antalya. She was still partly traumatized by the earthquake and vomited often during that ten-hour journey along the serpentine coastal road. She fainted at a rest stop. Six foreign children stood over her, looking worried. When she came around, a Turk held up her head.

"Take this," he said in perfect English, holding up a pill. She resisted; one doesn't take pills from strangers, not in Türkiye nor anywhere else.

"Don't worry Anna," he said. "It is I." Then she knew it was the Lord, took the pill, felt better, climbed back onto the bus, and safely delivered the children. A missionary couple took her in and tucked her into bed. When she eventually woke up her clothes, freshly washed, were neatly folded on a chair.

What else? We continued to lead Sunday morning worship services and mid-week prayer meetings for our team and continued to teach and monitor their progress in Turkish. I continued working on various writing projects and continued bussing to and from Istanbul to help with the new Christian magazine. However, life was an effort for the red fluid expanded until the thermometer burst and the liquid dribbled down the wall.

Summer passed. The trauma of the earthquake subsided as the aftershocks became milder and less frequent. The awful heat relented and those who'd fled to the sea or the mountains returned. Rita regained some weight. Soon we would be able to reach for a light blanket at night.

Then Anna got sick. Two weeks of frequent visits to the hospital, endless tests and a biopsy suggested something untoward. The Lord gave us quiet hearts as we prayed for grace to accept whatever he had in store for us. *"Shall we accept good from the Lord and not trouble?"* (Job 2:10). Still, we were thankful the results were cancer-negative.

Several times a week I pushed through bushes and brambles up a low hill where I'd sit with arms wrapped about my knees, my back resting against the bole of a gnarled olive tree. There, in the shade of its canopy, the wind sighing among the branches, I interceded for my family, for the city spread before me, for the Kurds, and for our team. When two other missionary couples began meeting regularly with a few local believers for worship and Bible study, I started interceding for them as well. The Spirit worked; several people were baptised in the lake, raising the total number of local believers to ten.

Today the city boasts several evangelical churches as well as a Christian bookstore.

Re-book your Tickets!

Jeremy Swan in Chad, 2024

It was less than two weeks until our flight home from Chad after nearly three years in Africa, when we received a phone call from the Canadian Ambassador in Cameroon, saying, "There is no way that we can get your son's passport issued and delivered to you in time. Contact your travel agent and re-book your flights." How could this be? We had been carefully working on paperwork to avoid this scenario ever since our son Jared's birth nearly two years earlier. What had gone wrong?

Our sixth child, Jared, was born in Chad about a year after we had arrived there for our second term. One of our teammates was a midwife from Germany who worked in a local clinic, so she had the ability to provide good care, but also to provide the necessary paperwork to begin the process of registering Jared's birth. With the document that the clinic provided, we were able to apply for a Chadian birth certificate.

While we were waiting for Jared's birth certificate, we took the 13-hour bus trip, 950 kilometres, from our home in Abéché to N'Djamena (the capital of Chad) for a time of rest. While we were there, we went to the Canadian consulate to begin the process of applying for Jared's Canadian citizenship. We were able to complete the application, except for the birth certificate, which they asked us to scan and email in upon our receipt. We received the certificate, scanned it, and sent it in by late April of 2022. We had been told that it would take about a year to process the citizenship request, but we were not planning to leave Chad until late 2023, so we just settled in to wait.

In April of 2023, we were again in N'Djamena, so we stopped in at the consulate to see if there was any word on our citizenship application. They told us that there wasn't, but that wait times were now 18 months, so this was normal. However, by the time that the 18 months would be up, we would have very little time until our planned trip to Canada, so we asked about getting a temporary passport while waiting for the citizenship to come through. "Yes, this could be done," they said, "but not six months ahead of time." Rather they recommended that we wait until within two months of travel and have our tickets reserved before applying, so that Passport Canada would recognize our situation as truly needing a temporary passport. We accepted this advice, but got passport photos taken for Jared while we were in N'Djamena, at the only studio we know of in the whole country that can take photos to the standards required for Canadian passports. Photos are valid for six months, so that would work fine.

In July, we finally received a notice from the Canadian immigration office, saying that Jared's application had been received in Nova Scotia in April of 2023, and that the wait time, now ten months, would start counting from that date. This was the first sign of trouble. Where had the application been for the first 12 months (April '22 to April '23)? It had needed to be sent from the consulate in N'Djamena to the Canadian embassy in Cameroon, and then be forwarded to the immigration office in Nova Scotia. This should have taken a matter of weeks, not a whole year!

We contacted the consulate again, saying that we now had a document indicating that Jared's citizenship would not be ready until sometime in 2024, and we were planning to travel in October 2023. "Can we apply for the temporary passport now?" we asked. "No, wait until late August, when you have your tickets," they said, "It is still too soon."

So, in late August, we compiled all the documents needed for the passport application, including the photos that had been taken at the beginning of April. We put everything in a big envelope, wrote on it the name and phone number of our co-workers who were in N'Djamena at the time, took it to the bus station, and gave it to the driver to deliver to the bus station in

N'Djamena. (There is no postal service in Chad, so sending documents by bus is a reasonable alternative.) However, when our co-workers went to the bus station to get the envelope, they were told that it was not there. Several phone calls were made to no avail. Finally, I went back to the bus station in our city (although I was sick with Dengue fever and could barely stand up) and talked to the man I had given it to. He called his contact on the other end, and was able to describe the envelope well enough that it could be found. Our co-workers picked up the envelope, delivered it to the consulate, and were assured that everything was in order, the passport should be ready in about six weeks.

A consulate does not have the authority to issue passports, so the application needed to be sent to the embassy in Cameroon to be processed, and then the passport would be sent back to Chad once it was issued. After the six weeks, I called the consulate in Chad to see if they had received the passport. They said, "No, but it will be fine." I asked, as I had several times before, what would happen if we reached the capital a few days before our flight and there was no passport; could they issue a travel document on the spot that would be sufficient? I was assured that yes, there would be no problem.

The next day, the consulate called me back, saying that a document was missing for the passport application. I quickly sent a scan of the needed document, but also realized that this meant that all was not going as expected, since the passport should have been not only issued, but delivered to Chad by this point. Further questioning revealed that the application had only been received at the embassy that week. At this point I contacted the ambassador directly to try and find out what was going on. When she called me back, the first thing she told me was, "I am sorry, but there is no way that you will be able to fly a week from Monday, you need to look into re-booking while we work to get Jared a passport. It will not be possible to do it in time."

I knew that rebooking eight round-trip tickets for our family would not be cheap, so I began asking questions, and together with the ambassador, we realized that if everything worked out perfectly, there was a slight chance that the passport would be ready in Cameroon by the next Friday. We would just need to arrange a way to get it to N'Djamena ourselves at that point. The number of things that would have to fall into place was daunting, and the obstacles looked impossible. To be honest, it would require a miracle for us to travel as planned. If the miracle didn't happen, we would be faced with a choice between re-booking all of our tickets, at a cost of $5000, or one of us taking the older five children to Canada while the other waited with Jared for the passport.

My conversation with the ambassador happened on the Friday before Thanksgiving, and we were to fly on a Monday night, one week after Thanksgiving. So, nothing would happen in any offices until after the long weekend, and then the time difference meant that the passport office in Canada and the Embassy in Cameroon were only open at the same time for about half of each day for the four working days of that week.

Our plan was to make a whole new passport application, but the passport photos that we had taken in April were now a few days more than six months old, and no longer valid. As I mentioned, there is only one studio in Chad that can make passport photos at Canadian standards, and it is in N'Djamena. We would not be able to finish packing and get to N'Djamena in time to get new photos. One of our teammates is a good photographer, so we rigged up a white background, took some photos, and sent them by email to the embassy, along with a letter explaining that we were unable to meet the normal requirements for passport photos. Thankfully, with the ambassador's help, the passport office was persuaded to accept these photos.

So, the application process was begun on Tuesday, with everything being sent in by email, and we finished packing and got on the bus early Wednesday morning to travel to N'Djamena. About halfway there, I got a text from the ambassador, saying that the application was complete, but I needed to pay for the passport online before she could send it to the passport office to be processed. I got onto the website for payment using the connection through my cell phone, and had just reached the last step of the payment process when the bus got far enough from the nearest town that I lost the connection, and the payment failed. Over the next half hour or so, I worked my way through the process again, doing one or two steps each time that we passed close enough to a cell tower to get online. The payment finally went through just a few minutes before the passport office in Canada was to open. Praise the Lord, we had the maximum possible time for them to work on our application.

Imagine our delight when I received another message from the ambassador as we were arriving in N'Djamena, saying that the application had been approved, so she had been able to issue the passport, and it was sitting on her desk, ready to go. It had only taken a few hours, instead of a couple of days, as we expected.

Now, to get it to Chad. I had no contacts in Cameroon, so I considered flying there myself to get it, but I asked in a chat group of mission leaders in Chad whether anyone did have contacts in Cameroon who could help. One man put me in touch with a missionary in the capital city who was a tremendous help, and together we made a plan. He sent a trusted taxi driver to the embassy on Thursday morning to get the passport and deliver it to a Cameroonian doctor who was to fly to a hospital in northern Cameroon on Friday. This was still a day's drive from N'Djamena, but I had a good Chadian friend who was willing to travel down to the hospital and pick it up. If all went well, we could have the passport in our hands by Saturday night—48 hours to spare.

The first problem came when the doctor's flight was delayed until Saturday, cutting into our grace period. Still, we sent our friend off on Saturday morning, travelling in a sort of inter-city taxi, just a small car on unimproved roads. He should reach the hospital Saturday night, spend the night in a hotel, and return on Sunday. About halfway there, disaster struck! The car hit a rock, resulting in a huge gash in its oil pan. It was not going any farther, and my friend had to endure a painful ride on the luggage rack of a motorcycle to the nearest town for the night. It was no longer possible for him to reach the hospital and return in time. It looked like we would have to give up. We were out of ideas and out of time.

God wasn't finished yet, though, and neither were our friends. Together with the Cameroonian doctor, my stranded friend came up with a plan. The doctor took the passport to the taxi station in his city, and entrusted the passport to a driver who was making the trip to N'Djamena on Sunday morning. He also reserved a seat, so that the taxi could pick up my friend halfway to complete the delivery. Their plan worked perfectly, and we finally had the passport in our hands by Sunday evening.

But the story still wasn't over. When we shared the good news with the mission community in Chad, who had been praying for us throughout this time, one person responded saying that she had also once received a passport shortly before leaving Chad, and was required to get an exit visa in it in order to leave the country. We asked the ambassador if this would be the case for us. She didn't know, but asked the consul in Chad. He didn't know either, so he contacted the immigration office first thing Monday morning. He was told that yes, we would need the exit visa, so he called me and said, "Come right away to the immigration office, bring the passport, and I will meet you there." At the office, the consul took care of everything, but it still took several hours. At one point they told him that they could fine us over $10,000 for Jared being in the country without a visa since he was born, but thankfully they did not.

Finally, at around 4:00 p.m., we had the visa in the passport and everything was in order. I had just enough time to get back to the guest house, pick up the family and our luggage, have supper, and get to the airport for our midnight flight. God still does amazing miracles, but it can be stressful watching them happen.

They were Looking for Guns

Jeremy Swan in Chad, 2023

"That must be the water delivery guy," I thought when I heard the loud knock at the gate to our courtyard very early one morning. We had told him to knock loudly. We certainly didn't want to miss water delivery in this dry land that is Chad. And, we didn't mind getting up early. The morning is the best time to get things done, before the heat sets in. I jumped out of bed to go to the gate. The knock seemed a little more insistent than usual. Maybe he was in a hurry today.

It wasn't the water delivery guy. At the gate, I was confronted with a group of soldiers in fatigues, with rifles on their shoulders. They let me know they were searching for guns.

Our neighbours had told us about soldiers visiting them yesterday. We had been away and were glad to have missed the excitement. The soldiers were doing a door-to-door search throughout the entire city looking for illegal weapons among civilians. And now they were back to look through the houses they had missed the previous day.

It was obvious that they were quite taken aback to have a white man answer the door, something they weren't expecting, but they had their orders to search the houses. By this time Melissa had thrown a skirt on over her PJ's so she was ready by the time they reached the house.

Without further ado, the soldiers walked right into the house still wearing their big army boots. Chadian always take off their shoes—usually flip-flops—before going into a house. The men were followed by a commander in charge of their group who did stoop down to untied his boots and take them off before entering. The soldiers looked around the kitchen and then the office obviously very uncomfortable and very hesitant to disturb anything we had. The kids were still in bed which caused them some embarrassment.

The commander urged his men to be a little more thorough, "You must open the things." They had to look inside the suitcases and storage boxes.

"What's in that box? What's in this box? We have to do a good job here." They even took apart our bedding just to see if there was anything under the sheets. All the while, they were very polite making their investigation seem like a simple formality.

Our house is laid out as one room after another, you have to go through each room to get to another. They were amazed at how far back the house went, definitely a little different than a typical Chadian house.

We had heard rumours that when soldiers search, they sometimes take valuables. So, Melissa stayed in the office where we had our money. I kept up with the lead group as they went from room to room. They couldn't have been in the house more than ten minutes. Nevertheless, it felt weird having some eight, armed soldiers search through our house. This is very different from what we experience in Canada.

Basking in His Presence

Ruth in East Asia, 2003

My house is full of excitement, noise and laughter. We just got back from dinner out. Thirty youth and I ate our fill of hotpot. They are getting good at telling me which parts in the hotpot I really do not want to eat. How could I not be filled with joy to hear their questions and know that they are talking more and more about our Lord?

Laughter spreads through the place and more young people come each time. It's a place where love resides and safety for the soul overrides any potential danger. This is a home away from home for so many. Even the parents often come to bask in the Lord's powerful presence.

A Little Child Shall Lead Them

Anonymous workers in Asia, 2023

At a school assembly the principal asked our six-year-old son to come up on the stage with him. When he was asked, our son didn't know the principal would be leading the whole school in worship to the goddess of education and arts. The principal bowed and all the children followed, except our little boy.

Later when questioned by his teacher, our son stood with his hands at his side in front of the whole class and said, "I only worship God."

The principal shared this story with us. He was obviously impressed with our son's forthright approach and respectful nature.

A Close Call

Walter Mohr in Indonesia, 1965

As daylight faded, two military police Jeeps stopped near our front door. Military police with white helmets and rifles quickly took up positions in front of our house and our neighbour's house. We were blocked in.

Fortunately for us, the soldiers knocked on our neighbour's door. He wasn't home. His life was spared, at least for the moment. We knew a soldier lived next door. We had chatted briefly but did not know him well. He was mostly on duty. We learned later that he was accused of being a communist.

The communist coup had failed. The party had been outlawed. It was now dangerous to be in any way associated with that party. It was not always so. The party had become amazingly popular in the early 1960's. It claimed more members than any other party. We were uneasy as we witnessed the growth of the party. We saw them gain seats in parliament. We saw the huge hammer and sickle signs on almost every street. We admired their discipline and commitment. When the communist party members paraded by, they were organized and disciplined. Three months previously they were adored at every level of government. To speak negatively of them would have meant expulsion from the country.

I sighed in relief as the military police drove away. I also saw instantly how different it could have ended. What if they had knocked on our door. What if they had done a search. Our house had many communist books. Some were given to me by dedicated believers in communism. Others I had purchased.

I had studied these books. I had underlined key phrases. Not because I loved them or believed them. I was trying to understand what drew so many people to their cause. Even Christians who were faithful in attending our meetings were praising them. When I tried to warn these Christians, I was told that Indonesian communism was tolerant and there would be freedom of religion.

I was amazed at how well the communists understood people's needs; how glowing their promises; and how they organized every segment of society to help them reach their goal. They would create a better world. I admired their zeal and devotion to their cause. If only I could inspire such devotion in new Christians.

That evening, I cleaned house. I tore up my communist books and literature. I shredded the pages into little pieces and threw them down the bathroom squat toilet. As usual, I covered the hole with a board. No one would go checking for banned books in the toilet.

This was a warning to me. Be careful about what you gather and store up. Incriminating evidence could be deadly.

V

Despite Persecution

Blessed are those who are persecuted because of righteousness, for theirs is the kingdom of heaven. Blessed are you when people insult you, persecute you and falsely say all kinds of evil against you because of me. Rejoice and be glad, because great is your reward in heaven, for in the same way they persecuted the prophets who were before you.
Matthew 5:10-12

Sometimes a missionary is persistently harassed, oppressed, or persecuted. Jesus says that person is blessed and in good company. Great is your reward in heaven.
When Walter Mohr and Miranda Meikle were going through trials, and learning spiritual lessons here on earth, they were also earning rewards in heaven. When Ruth faced the fire, she was being set up for a heavenly blessing. When Ralph with his Bibles and books were thrown into the river, God used that in his grand scheme. These saints may not have been thinking about the blessing at the time, but you can be sure they were trusting their Heavenly Father to take them through.

Hallelujah Street

Walter Mohr in Indonesia, 1964

As young inexperienced missionaries, just two years into our venture, we found ourselves living in a remote suburb of the city of Madiun. We had developed friendly relationships with most of our near neighbours. However, to exit our neighbourhood we needed to turn a corner and drive 500 metres along Treng Street, a narrow street with houses close to each other on both sides and where we did not know anyone. Treng Street connected us to the wider main street leading to the main city shops. Getting to almost anywhere, even to our church services, meant a drive on Treng Street.

One mid-January morning a child on Treng Street thought it would be fun to shout hallelujah as we passed by. At first, I was amused. I don't know how hallelujah became the word for us. Perhaps occasionally, if something really good happened I might have uttered a hallelujah. It simply means praise God. And I had many reasons to praise him. But I cannot think of a time when someone living on Treng Street, some distance from our home, would have heard me use this word.

Within days, children all along that street were shouting hallelujah as I passed by on our scooter. What made it worse, parents sitting on the front steps of their homes had big smiles on their faces as the children shouted. Every time hallelujahs conducted us up the entire street. This became overwhelmingly irritating. I felt that God and I were being dishonoured and disrespected. In response I drove faster than usual, head down, eyes fixed on the road ahead. I ignored the smiling faces on either side of the street. I'm sure everyone—children and adults—sensed my discomfort which increased their amusement. For me this became a major embarrassment. Just being the only white people around brought enough unwanted attention, we certainly did not need this extra publicity.

I found another somewhat inconvenient way to get to the main areas of the city. There was a narrow, crowded path that hardly counted as a street. A short stretch of that path was actually a small local village market. Goods were spread out along the edge. To pass I needed to dismount and push the scooter through and around the fruits and vegetables laid out for sale. It was a slower, more difficult way to get out of our area but no one here shouted hallelujah. When I drove alone this worked reasonably well but when Melita came with me, usually holding baby Philip in her arms, it was very uncomfortable. We were unknown in that area so there was lots of staring and we could hear whispers about us being Dutch or white. But I was avoiding what I thought of as harassment, perhaps even mild persecution.

This carried on for some weeks—eroding my joy. Then one morning during my devotions, these verses jumped out at me: *"Love your enemies, do good to those who hate you. Bless those who curse you, pray for those who mistreat you"* (Luke 6:27-8). I felt convicted. God was speaking directly to me. These folk on Treng street did not hate me, they were not my enemies, they were not cursing me. They probably had no idea what hallelujah meant. Jesus died for them just as he did for all those living near me. They were simply having a bit of fun and I was not acting in a very Christlike manner. How could I show love? How could I do good?

I confessed my sinful attitude and asked for God's forgiveness. Here I was, a missionary called to love these people and reach them with the gospel, acting unchristian, avoiding and hiding from them. I vowed that morning that I would quit using the narrow market path and again drive along Treng street as I had in previous months.

How well I remember the drive that morning. Humanly speaking nothing changed. Smiling, happy faces filled the air with hallelujahs just as before.

But for me it was different. I did not speed along with my head bowed low, bearing this trial. I put a smile on my face and a prayer in my heart. I looked at the faces, both to the right and to the left, acknowledging everyone. And I did it again the next day and the next day—sometimes waving to show my friendliness. I conveyed a very different message.

Perhaps it looked like I enjoyed this too much and making me happy was not a goal. So, in a matter of days or at best a week or two, the hallelujah shouts died out. I felt we were seeing friends as we drove that street. God loved these people. Christ died for them. Over time some did become friends and I recall one day a man beckoned me asking that I come into his house. They had a sick child, would I pray? Of course, I would pray. I would also come back to ask about the child and pray again.

That silly little trial taught me a valuable lesson. Do not flee from difficulties. Face them. Ask God for wisdom and grace. Overcome the trial. Use it to glorify the Lord. Hallelujah street helped make me a better missionary.

Psalm 16

Miranda in West Africa, 2008

"Keep me safe, my God, for in you I take refuge. I say to the Lord, 'You are my Lord; apart from you I have no good thing.' I say of the holy people who are in the land, 'They are the noble ones in whom is all my delight.' Those who run after other gods will suffer more and more. I will not pour out libations of blood to such gods or take up their names on my lips. Lord, you alone are my portion and my cup; you make my lot secure. The boundary lines have fallen for me in pleasant places; surely, I have a delightful inheritance. I will praise the Lord, who counsels me; even at night my heart instructs me. I keep my eyes always on the Lord. With him at my right hand, I shall not be shaken. Therefore, my heart is glad and my tongue rejoices; my body also will rest secure, because you will not abandon me to the realm of the dead, nor will you let your faithful one see decay. You make known to me the path of life; you will fill me with joy in your presence, with eternal pleasures at your right hand."

In December 2008 I returned to West Africa as a missionary after having been evacuated from there for a strange health crisis that seemed to be a form of spiritual attack. It was deemed unwise for me to return to my previous living situation in a Muslim village where four days of the week I was the only worker, only Christian, only white person. I loved this village deeply (still do), and it was hard to let it go.

It was also hard to know where I should be. I was still doing language learning, and a young single woman. After some months of thinking through various options, it was proposed that I move to Ndara, a city that was the former capital. We had no WEC team there, but another team of American missionaries was living there. The only mature Christian couple from the people group I wanted to reach (the Wolof) had been asked if they would accept me into their home and family, and they had agreed. There was one girl, Seynabou, who had been a good friend of mine in the village who had married into a family in Ndar and she was the only person I knew there.

After thinking and praying about this option, the Lord spoke to me through Psalm 16 to confirm that this was indeed his way forward for me. I was looking to God to keep me safe, particularly after my previous near-death experience which had caused my return to Canada. I understood that delighting in the "holy ones" in the land referred to living with this Christian Wolof family.

So, in February 2009 I moved to Ndar with the intention of living there for a year. I went back to the village I had been living in to collect my things. My local friend, Mbooy, helped me to pack, arranged transportation, and came with me to Ndar for two days to help me settle. I begged her to stay longer, and she stayed another night but then needed to return to her family. I cried myself to sleep that first night without her; I felt so lonely and alone. But before she left, we had located our friend Seynabou and I now knew how to get to where she was living in Ndar, quite a distance from where I was.

Seynabou had married one of the sons of an important imam (Muslim religious leader) in Ndar. Her husband, Sidi, was the oldest son of the third wife (Muslim men are permitted four wives), and they lived in a large house that housed the imam's four wives, their sons and their sons' wives, and the grandchildren. It was a rich household, by local standards, but not a happy one, full of intrigue between the wives and their children, and a strong pecking order with those more recently married-in living as servants to the older women. Seynabou, although happy with her husband, was deeply unhappy in her living situation and rejoiced to receive me as her guest, not just for my company, but for the honour my presence as a white person brought to her. I thought that it must be for the sake of Seynabou that God had moved me to Ndar.

However, on my second visit to the house, one of the half-brothers of her husband found me in a room talking to the women and sat down next to me, a little too close, and started making me feel very uncomfortable. I soon left, as it was about time for me to return home. But on my next visit the same thing happened; he found me with the women, sat down too closely and began touching me in inappropriate ways. One of the other women noticed how uncomfortable I was and told him off, but he just laughed as her words didn't carry much weight in a culture dominated by men. After the third time this happened, I told Seynabou I didn't feel I could visit her anymore, and could she please come to me at my house. Although she was permitted to visit once, her responsibilities at her house as one of the younger women doing all the cooking, cleaning and laundry, meant she didn't have time to come to me. She pleaded with me to continue to visit her, but rarely did I have enough courage to go.

When Fatima, the mother in my household, noticed I wasn't visiting Seynabou as much, she started introducing me to young women in the neighbourhood, girls I could practice language with and hopefully share the gospel with. One day as I was walking with two of them about a block from my house, they started screaming and ran off in different directions. A very deranged man in the street was running after me. Thankfully I was close to the compound of the extended family of Madou, the father of my household, and I ran in there. Hearing all the commotion, members of the household came out of their rooms and the grandfather chased the man off with a stick. No one knew who the man was or what he was doing in the neighbourhood, but everyone assured me he surely hadn't meant any harm and it wouldn't happen again. Unfortunately, in the next few weeks, two more similar incidents occurred with different men in the neighbourhood, one a very drunk brick-layer, and the other looking like he was demon-possessed.

Another friend I had made, a local girl who attended the church, offered to take me on walks out of the neighbourhood, closer to where she lived. But on those walks children started throwing things at me and insulting me. My friend, FaDiop, threatened to tell their parents on them for their shameful behaviour, but it didn't seem to have much lasting effect. After a few walks like this she stopped asking me to go on walks with her.

I tried to talk to Fatima and another older single missionary in the same city about what I was experiencing, but they dismissed it as 'kids being kids' and 'wrong place, wrong time,' or perhaps I wasn't dressed appropriately, or acting culturally appropriate. One day I was going to church for a prayer meeting and Bible study. There was a large open sandy space in front of the church and young men in their late teens, early twenties were playing soccer there. Three of them were on the sidelines sitting on the steps leading up to the church. As I climbed the steps of the church, behind Madou and in front of Fatima, I suddenly heard Fatima start berating someone and Madou and I turned around to see what was going on. One of the young men had been reaching out to touch me inappropriately and Fatima had seen it and started yelling at him the moment before he actually touched me. From then on, she understood what I had been experiencing but didn't know what to do about it, other than to encourage me to stay home.

But I wasn't particularly comfortable inside their home. They were a lovely family, but the room I lived in was old and falling apart. It had a corrugated tin roof which meant when the sun came out it was incredibly hot. There was no screen on the window and people walking on the road would sometimes toss garbage in, whether because they knew it was my room, or because it looked like a place to toss garbage, I didn't really know. I started shutting the corrugated tin shutters during the day, but this of course made it even hotter and stuffier, and still didn't hinder the sand being whipped in by the wind. The family had informed me when I moved in that when they had enough money, they were planning to redo that room to make it as nice as the rest of the house. I was of course free to spend time in other parts of the house, but the noise and antics of their three boys made it hard to study. I was desperate for time to myself, not immersed in a foreign language and culture.

As part of the arrangement for living far from any WEC team, I was expected to travel to the capital once a month to attend a WEC team meeting. In some ways I looked forward to the chance to leave Ndar, but the travelling itself was rather challenging. It should have been a four-hour trip by public transportation, but the capital is located on a peninsula something like a tail on a fish, and everyone anywhere in the country trying to get to the capital had to pass through a narrow stretch, which quite obviously produced major traffic jams. Sometimes I would be 45 kilometres from my final destination but sit there for an extra three hours. The vehicles I travelled in had been refitted to get the most passengers in, but part of that refitting somehow meant that the exhaust of the vehicle was piped back into the car at the back. When at a standstill and no wind flow, the result was sitting in a cloud of exhaust and heat. I was always sick and vomiting for the rest of the day, and the next day. Then I attended the team meeting, and the following day made the return trip, only to be sick again for the next day and a half.

After a few months of this, I was really struggling. Sometimes when I sat with my Bible it would fall open automatically to Psalm 16. In those days it was my habit to write notes in the margin of my Bible of things the Lord had said to me or verses he had given me. I would read through Psalm 16 and its talk of pleasant places and resting secure and wonder when those parts of my experience in Ndar were going to happen. Was I still just in the settling-in stage?

Or had God's promises to me failed?

It was during this time that we were praying for another one of our missionaries in another country. She had been kidnapped by religious fanatics. At one of the team meetings in the capital, we had set aside a special time to intercede for her. I was reading through passages about God *"rending the heavens and coming down."* And from the depths of my heart, I prayed to God, "If you truly are God, then rend the heavens and come down, release her, and I will know that you are still a God who cares!"

After 11 months of praying for her release, the following week I learned that she had been released, and as much as I know that was for her sake, it somehow also felt like it was for my sake. In all the years of my relationship with God, from the time I was five and first declared that I knew he was God, and I knew he was my God, I had never been so close to wanting to turn my back on him.

Not long after that, I was granted release from what had come to feel like my own captivity in Ndar. The family finally had enough money to begin constructing a new room and I didn't have to live there for the next few months while that was happening. A few months later my leadership decided I wouldn't return there to live.

My seven months of living in Ndar just about broke me. In the two years that followed, again and again my Bible would fall open to Psalm 16 and bitter questions of "Why this...?" and "Why that...?" would flood my heart. But most of all, "God why would you promise pleasant places and delightful inheritance and joy, but then give me the opposite?" As I wrestled through those questions honestly and oftentimes with deep anger, I felt God say to me again and again, "Yes, I was behind all those circumstances. Yes, I sent you to Ndar knowing all that would happen. Yes, I sent you there with the promises of Psalm 16."

And I again came to a place of needing to decide would I turn my back on God? I could never deny that he existed, I had had far too much of a relationship, too many conversations, to deny his existence.

But his goodness...could I trust his goodness? God never gave any explanations, not for my time in Ndar, not for the experiences leading up to it. I wanted desperately to make sense of it, to be able to say this happened so that that could happen, but God never gave me that option. All he said to me was: "Trust me. I am good."

And I made the choice, as foolhardy as it felt in that moment, to say, "Yes, I will trust you."

And that has made all the difference. God began to dismantle lies I had held about who he was and how he was obligated to work in the world and in my life. He dismantled lies I held about myself and what it meant to be a missionary and serve him. These were the gods that Psalm 16 talked about that brought more and more suffering.

And as he did that work in my life, step by step I entered into my delightful inheritance having deep joy in his presence. In later years I faced circumstances and situations far more challenging than those I had faced in Ndar, but never again did I step outside the boundary lines that he had placed for me in pleasant places, for of course this was not merely a physical place, but a spiritual one, one that cannot be taken away.

Saved from the Fire

Ruth in East Asia, 2000's

One evening, while I was cooking, the sleeve of my sweater caught fire in the gas burner. The flames shot high and I had no time to do anything. I believed someone was praying for me, as just as suddenly as they started, the flames went out. For a moment I thought I had imagined the flames, but when I smelled the fibres of my sweater, they smelled burnt, but not a hair on my arm or a thread of the sweater was burned.

I found out later, a friend from Canada had been moved to wake up and pray for me early in the morning. It was at the exact time the flames went up. I was cooking at six in the evening and she awoke to pray at six in the morning. Our God is amazing.

This was not the only time God saved me from fire. One time I was preparing for bed and turned on my electric blanket. I usually read in bed but this night something on television had my attention. I watched for a while but got cold so went to the bedroom to get a sweater. The room was filled with smoke and when I lifted the edge of the covers, the bed burst into flames. The locals in my community still talk about the one whose God could control fire and protect them. I lived in an area of the Y people and to them their fire god was the strongest. Yet here was a God that overwhelmed the will of the fire god.

Once a year the Y people have a night of fire festivities to honour their fire god. All the young people carry brooms on fire and wave them around. It was widely known that my God had saved me from the fire in my bed. That might be why a group of young people surrounded me with their brooms and the leader kept poking his broom at me. I admit I was afraid for a moment but then I knew God was with me. The fiery broom came closer and closer. Then it touched me and extinguished. A hush followed. I smiled as I walked on. Indeed, hearts were touched.

Torrential Baptism

Ralph Hines in Colombia, 1953

As our dugout canoe touched on the broad flat beach at Cambao, Hipolito Diaz, a native believer, and I stepped on shore to be confronted by a group of six men. We had seen them as we crossed the Magdalena River and hoped they were planning to have a swim. This was not to be. Two were in police uniform and the others in civilian clothes. Before we could take six steps, we were ordered to stop and be searched. The contents of our pockets were examined and returned to us. Then my briefcase was opened and my Bible and hymnbook were violently thrown to the ground. We were in trouble.

We had come to Cambao that 28th day of December with high hopes of holding our first evangelical baptism service. Hipolito an elder of the church in Honda and a lay preacher had carefully prepared the believers. Old Jose, his wife and daughter Rufina were expected to be ready for their baptism.

The little group of believers had suffered persecution and many threats; ever since the gospel meetings had first been held there some three years before. Some had turned back but others had stood firm and were ready to face anything the Lord permitted.

We had not used the government ferry that day, though it was free for all who wished to cross the river. Three months previously, when Martha and I had visited Cambao, one of the ferry men had been insulting. "Come back and we will give you a ride and a bath!" he called out as we left the ferry. So, we ceased using the ferry and arranged for boys of the Urquijo family to meet us up river, with the canoe.

I was sorry to leave Martha at home in Honda that morning. She had wanted to go with me and take our four-year-old daughter, Caroline, too. Caroline had taken sick with a nasty mouth infection just before Christmas. It had dampened the spirits of an otherwise happy day. Now it was obvious that God was in our apparent disappointment. Now I was on my own and it was best.

The men began insulting us, using foul language and accusing us of filling the town with our doctrines. Then while a policeman questioned me; the Inspector of Police came behind me and struck me twice across the back with his walking stick. My hat flew off and my glasses bounced about so I removed them and stuck them in my pocket. "You're going into the river, do you hear?" shouted the inspector. "This is a Catholic town and the Conservatives are in power." Then he followed up with filthy and insulting accusations too vile to repeat. The inspector turned to Hipolito, struck him twice across the back with his cane and knocked him down with two blows to his face. This was followed by several brutal kicks and more abusive speech.

Quickly another man brought one of our hymnbooks to me and ordered me to burn it. Thoroughly frightened, but thankful that it wasn't the Bible, I made an appearance at attempting to put fire to it. When it didn't burn, they gathered all our books and threw them into the river.

"Now into the river you go. Get out of here!" they ordered. Leading me to the water's edge they pushed me in. With revolver in hand, the policeman also ordered Hipolito into the river. Threatening to shoot us, he commanded that we throw ourselves full length into the water. There was nothing to do but obey orders. We plunged in. Soon we were submerged to our necks, fully clothed, shoes and all. Farther and farther, we went into the swiftly flowing stream. Our tormentors were watching us intently. Since neither of us were good swimmers, we had to trust God to work for us.

Although there had not been rain in our district for many days, somewhere it must have rained because the swollen mountain streams had brought down some banana trees. Three of these entangled in a tough vine were caught on a rock just upstream from where we were driven into the river. Using the vine and a cord, Hipolito had kept from his parcel of books, he was able to bind the three trees together side by side. Stretching ourselves out on our makeshift raft, we pushed off and were carried downstream. At first, we paddled with our arms but soon tired and lay quietly while the swift current carried us along.

We floated for quite a distance and then a current pulled us into our homeward shore. The place we landed was like a tangled jungle and we could not walk far, but a fisherman in a dugout canoe came along, saw our dripping clothes, and in sympathy took us to a place where we could get onto a road and walk to the train station.

Meanwhile Martha had hired a car and began a frantic search for us. God graciously worked some miracles, various phone calls were made, and she learned that we had arrived in Mariquita. Soon Martha and I were joyfully in one another's arms recounting the Lord's mercies.

When the Governor was informed of the attack, he sent a special investigator who confirmed our report, whereupon the Inspector of Police was dismissed and the policeman was sent elsewhere.

Two months later Hipolito and I returned to the place where we had been driven into the river. There we baptized the three believers. Through persecution, God continues to work in Colombia.

The Troublesome Tract

Walter Mohr in Indonesia, 1973

'*You do not need religion. Religion cannot help you.*' In most countries this phrasing would not be a problem. To us the intent was clear, religion does not save. Jesus saves from sin. Little did we know that government officials in Indonesia in 1973 would read something sinister in these words. The backlash on our ministry was severe.

Operation Mobilization had used a publisher in Java to print up the three million tracts entitled, "Seven things you need to know!" to be handed out in co-ordination with a visit of their Logos ship. Then, just before the ship was to arrive, permission to dock was cancelled and the visit could not happen.

At the time, I was supposed to be on furlough in Canada but just happened to be in Java to extend our visas and to attend the annual WEC conference. I got a welcome message from my friend, the publisher of these tracts, "No expense to you, just come and get as many tracts as you want." I was excited, took out the middle seat in the van and drove to the place of publication in Surabaya. I loaded up two heavy big boxes—112,000 tracts plus 300 Gospels. I knew that literature printed by Operation Mobilization would be doctrinally sound. The salvation message could reach into thousands of homes. Hopefully many hearts would be enlightened and perhaps hundreds would find salvation in Christ.

The Christians in Madiun joined in the excitement. It meant that, along with the usual market visits and literature sales, we could distribute this tract and freely give out the small gospels. In fact, we would make these visits a priority so the message would reach far and wide. The very next day we made our first outreach to an area far to the south of our city. We had a good reception. Our outreach continued. Almost daily we visited different areas and all went well. About 12,000 tracts were distributed.

After three weeks we had our first encounter with the police. We were well known in the area so thought nothing of it. Policemen often watched us as we sold books and preached in the open air. Some even bought books and accepted tracts. We continued our outreach for another week. Then I was unexpectedly summoned to a nearby sub-district police station. To my consternation every person who had been with me on that outreach a week earlier was also at the police station. However, I was not allowed to speak to them. They were taken to a different area for questioning. You can be sure they were even more anxious and fearful than I was.

I was taken to a small cubicle at the police station and given a chair next to a small table. I wondered what was happening. A grim-faced policemen entered and placed a copy of the tract, with the offending two sentences heavily underlined, on the table. He handed me a sheet of paper and instructed me to write an explanation of the meaning of these sentences. He left.

Suddenly the two sentences looked frightening. In Indonesia religion is compulsory. Every Indonesian must carry a citizenship card with their religion listed. This provocative statement that religion was not important stared at me. Then I also realized the title page of the tract was red—not a helpful colour. Communist signs had been red. Though the party had been outlawed 12 years earlier, the fear of that dreaded atheistic teaching was still very real. Was I suspected of being a secret communist? I was almost certain that this was the frightening implication.

I prayed and meditated, read and reread the whole tract, and with God's help wrote an explanation. I simply retold the seven steps to salvation that were outlined so well in this tract. But I also emphasized that I myself was certainly religious. I was not anti-religion. In fact, I followed the Christian religion. However, I pointed out that my religion, or any religion cannot save from sin and damnation. As the tract clearly stated, only Jesus saves. After some hours my written explanation was taken from me and I was released and told that I was free to go home.

I was hesitant to leave. I feared for my Indonesian friends. After several more hours of waiting, they too were released. They were quite shaken. During their interrogation they had been warned that I might be a communist sympathizer—who else in Indonesia would dare to attack religion? After I drove them to their home area some distance away, we stopped and read Acts 4:23-31, then prayed together. Now consider their threats and enable your servants to speak your word with boldness.... Just as those early followers of Jesus had prayed, we also lifted our voices and concerns to God. Praise God, none of those men left Jesus—all continued steadfast in faith. I believe their faith was strengthened.

For me this was just the beginning of an extended season of trial. Our Madiun church leaders also came under scrutiny and some were questioned at the district police office. Shortly thereafter several policemen came to our house with an order to confiscate the remaining 100,000 tracts. I was asked to sign a document confessing that I had committed a crime and was willingly surrendering the tracts. I was told that I might need to revisit all the villages in which these tracts were scattered and try to recall as many as possible. Thankfully they did not follow through on that suggestion. It would have been an impossible task.

In the weeks that followed I was called to religious offices as well as various police stations. Clearly, in the view of high-ranking persons this little tract was a major issue. I was summoned to the police station in the city where the tracts were printed. Of course, I had no knowledge of printing details. I was then told that I would be kept under surveillance and would not be allowed to leave Indonesia until this case was satisfactorily settled.

Fortunately, a week later, when I was scheduled to return to Canada I was not hindered or questioned. I felt like a bird freed from its cage. When the airplane left the Jakarta airport, I was soaring high, leaving my troubles behind. Others affected by this were not so fortunate. I learned from afar that this case was discussed at the highest levels of government. There was a prolonged investigation. All who were in any way involved—the person who translated the tract, the one who proofread the tract, the publisher and printer of the tract—were questioned. The blame probably rested with the translator who had not foreseen the damage this word could cause. Perhaps he translated too literally from an English tract. But all others, including myself, were negligent in not having examined the tract more carefully before distributing it.

After prolonged investigations the case was dropped. No charges were laid. No one served time in prison. A link to communism was not established. I presume the stockpile of tracts were destroyed. But for me, and for many other well-meaning Christians, this was a painful ordeal. This experience taught me to handle the term religion with care. In Indonesia it carries great significance.

VI

Evangelizing

He (Jesus) said to them, "Go into all the world and preach the gospel to all creation...."
Mark 16:15

Missionaries evangelize. There are opportunities everywhere. Often, God sets up the moment in time and space as an answer to a simple prayer. It could be at a birthday party, in a tea garden or in the home of an absent Muslim teacher. It could take place by invitation into an unbeliever's home or at a Muslim sacrificial ceremony or through a tract found in the garbage or even in a mosque. With God, surprises abound.

A Birthday Party

Fred in the Middle East, 2021

On the way to see my friend who lives in a city in the north of the country, I wanted to visit a few other nearby provinces. I chose to stay at a city of about 150 thousand where there was no apparent Christian fellowship.

As I wandered around this city, I decided to hitchhike up to a large statue at the top of a mountain. I prayed for the Lord to have someone pick me up who he wanted me to talk to—immediately a young fellow pulled over. He said that he didn't have much time because he had just come back from university and his brother was having a combination birthday party and welcome back party for him. He said he could take me to the mountaintop, take a few pictures and then drive me back to the centre of the city.

Afterwards, on the way to the city centre, I asked about the location of the best restaurant. He took me to a burger place which I enjoyed. Despite having no time, he sat with me, introduced me to several other people he knew, and generously paid for my meal. Then instead of leaving me in the city he took me to the party. There he invited me to stay the night.

About three in the morning, we were playing video games. I left Bible college years ago and thought I had left the culture of video games behind, but here I was at three a.m. doing that very thing in a cloud of cigarette smoke. The friends finally left and I was able to claim the couch.

As we were getting the bed ready, my new friend and I started talking more about Christ. I asked if he had a Bible. He just happened to have ordered a Bible online and was trying to meet up with someone to explain more to him. He was in contact with a friend of mine, but it never worked out to meet.

The Lord had arranged my weekend stay at his house to share the good news. Then because my new friend had been researching, he was able to help me explain some difficult Christian concepts, like the Trinity, to his family. They all heard the gospel and were encouraged. God is amazing.

A Spiritual Battle

Karli in the Middle East, 2015

Karli in a Middle Eastern country, has been praying that the Lord would lead her to a tea garden where she could meet with women and practise speaking their language. There are many tea gardens where she is but they tend to be full of men and not a comfortable place for a woman to sit. Then the Lord showed her the perfect tea garden, which she began visiting frequently. Each time she went, single women or groups of women have come and asked if they can sit at her table.

Although she had the opportunity to have long conversations with women she meets elsewhere—opportunities that have opened the way for her to talk about the Lord, there have been no such opportunities at the tea garden. When no door opened to talk of the Lord, Karli cried out to the Lord, asking him to allow her to share with someone in the garden.

The answer to her prayer came quickly when an older woman in the full black burqa came and asked if she could sit with her. After a few minutes of shallow conversation (generally Karli has trouble getting women wearing burqas to even smile at her), the woman asked Karli if she was Muslim. She replied no and explained that she loved Jesus.

"What does that mean?" the woman asked. "Are you a Muslim who loves Jesus?"

"No," Karli replied, "I suppose it means I am a Christian. But I don't pray to Mary and I am not Catholic and I think it is wrong to pray to Mary."

The woman replied that she was a Muslim and that she prayed five times a day. She then wanted to know when and how and to whom Karli prayed. These and other questions led Karli to share the complete gospel message with the woman. At one point the woman's daughter called her and the woman told her daughter, "I am just in the middle of talking to some kind of Jew! She reads the Injil (New Testament) and prays all the time and is a person of faith and she is telling me that she believes Jesus died on the cross to take the punishment for our sins and that Jesus is our hope. She believes in God. And she is wearing long sleeves!" Following, the phone call, the discussion with the woman continued. Karli says they ended up talking for about two and a half hours and that she was able to share the good news four or five times, each time in more depth, sometimes with tears. "You explain these things well, it makes sense," the woman told her at one point.

However, the discussion took a turn for the worse when the woman began to argue that Jesus is not the Son of God. Not being a fan of debate Karli would normally try to move on from that topic. But she clearly heard Jesus say, *"if you deny me before men I will deny you before my Father in heaven, tell her that I am Lord"* (Matt. 10:32). With much fear and trembling she declared, "Jesus is not only the Son of God, he is Lord!"

In that moment, Karli says something very, very demonic came over the Muslim woman. "Her eyes were filled with darkness and she completely turned on me. She began frantically reciting verses from the Quran, she was like a completely different person. I felt that I was in the midst of a very intense spiritual battle. In my mind I began to pray with all my might. She went on for quite a while, ranting, being angry with me and reciting many verses. Then suddenly I got a massive migraine headache. I did not tell her I had a headache and there is no way she could have known but she looked into my eyes and said, 'If you become a Muslim, you will be happy and your headache will go away.' This was obviously slightly freaky, but more than that it showed me that what was going on here was more spiritual then personal."

After about twenty more minutes, Karli said she knew the woman wouldn't listen further, so she told her she needed to leave but that God loved her and she would be praying for her. As Karli walked away, she said, Jesus is Lord, Jesus is Lord, Jesus is Lord was repeating in her mind and she began to weep for the woman.

As Karli walked away, she prayed, "Jesus, thank you that you are the way the truth and the life and that no one comes to the Father except through you. Father, in the name of Jesus I declare that I will never become a Muslim, Jesus is the truth and I ask you to heal my headache."

Immediately her intense headache went away.

When God Opens the Heart

Walter Mohr in Indonesia, 1967

Three days before Christmas 1967, Anwar, a keen Indonesian believer, and I rode our motorcycle into a well-known Islamic stronghold region. We were here at the invitation of a Muslim teacher who wanted us to visit his home and explain the gospel message. To be invited was in itself a most unlikely miracle. As arranged, we arrived early afternoon on the set date and at the set time to find his door open.

At the door, we repeatedly called out the usual Javanese greeting. There was no answer. Rather discouraged we began packing up preparing to leave. Then a few young men from across the street approached us. They explained that the teacher's wife had passed away suddenly and that he could not be home. Then they told us that they too were interested in what Christians believed and he had given permission to use his home.

Five young men in their later teens led us into that simple village home. An open door and a few small windows were our only light. We sat down on rattan chairs in circular fashion and introduced ourselves to each other. They all lived nearby and were eager to hear from real Christians.

I stood and unrolled a set of seven large pictures, the heart of man chart. I also held up my Bible before placing it on the small table. "This book," I said, "is the source of the good news I want to bring you today. It contains the Injil you all know about. This book tells us about God's great love for men and women all around the world." I told them God had called me and sent me here from Canada. I then shared the heart of man chart, one of my favourite tools in explaining the gospel. I had their attention. Their eyes were riveted on the pictures and on me.

I explained the first page in which the heart was black. "This," I said, "describes the darkness and power of sin and how Satan has blinded hearts and holds them in his grip." Then as I turned over page after page, I unfolded the good news that truth brings conviction and light; how the human heart tends to resist that light; how God's Spirit can penetrate and cast out the darkness; and how rejecting God's truth brings deeper darkness. I sensed they were fully engaged and attentive. God's Spirit was at work in their hearts.

I ended by sharing how Christ's death on the cross breaks the power of sin, brings forgiveness and assurance of heaven. "He is offering you new life as a free gift but each one must personally accept that gift." Then I sat down waiting for questions. No one spoke. I wondered if they really understood the message but asked if they wanted Jesus to change their hearts. Without hesitation three said they did. For Muslims to respond so quickly is highly unusual so I briefly recounted the gospel again.

Still unsure if they really fathomed the step they were taking and the gravity of this decision I suggested we kneel on the dirt floor and they simply tell Jesus what they had told me. All seven of us got down on our knees. Anwar led in an opening prayer thanking God for the great gift of salvation and forgiveness that was now waiting at the door of every heart. Then we waited. With faltering words one after another three young men confessed their sin and asked Jesus to save them. I concluded by thanking God for being in our midst, hearing our prayers and doing what he had promised.

What I will never forget is the radiance on Doddy's face when we rose to our feet. An hour ago, we were total strangers. Now his arms reached out to embrace me. He had met Jesus. A drastic change had happened. With excitement we arranged a follow-up visit and with happy hearts made our way back home. The follow-up visit never happened. Within a few days we received a message saying, "Please do not come. The whole village is in uproar. We are being threatened. Some of us will try to come to visit you but please do not come." And some did come, but not for long. Only Doddy persevered.

We understood the pressures they faced when we were given more details. Fear is a powerful force. They were facing severe persecution. The threats from village leaders included warnings that none of them would be allowed to marry a girl from their village, and none of them would ever have a burial plot in the local cemetery. These were major concerns for these young men. Not long after that Doddy's mother feeling the pressure and disgrace, despite this being her only son, demanded he leave the house. The father had left them years before.

So, Doddy came to Madiun carrying a few clothes and personal belongings. Thankfully the Madiun fellowship had recently rented a larger space for the growing community of believers and there were some empty storage rooms and a kitchen and washroom on the property at the back of the church. Doddy gladly accepted the accommodation we offered and was embraced by the Christians.

As we learned more of his background we could only marvel at the grace of God. He had been attending an Islamic school and knew that Jesus was a highly praised prophet. Also, how even though he heard only negative stories about Christians, the song Silent Night had strangely spoken to his heart. As Doddy became part of the fellowship, studied the Bible, and shared in the church services he grew quickly in the Lord.

Within a short time, Doddy was eagerly and boldly sharing his faith. We took him along on evangelistic outreaches to unreached villages and his testimony and witness was powerful. Not much later he testified of his sense of calling to be an evangelist and desire to give his life fully to making Jesus known. The church elders discussed his calling and approved him as one of the full-time workers who would be given financial support. Along with several others he would assist in ministry as churches were springing up in the Madiun area.

It was evident that his witness was bearing fruit. Within eleven months of his conversion Doddy came with excitement to tell us that he had led his mother to Jesus. She became one of his strongest supporters and of course welcomed him back home as often as he wished to come. For many years his village of Kebonsari resisted and strongly opposed the gospel but praise God a flourishing church now stands among them. Perhaps that school teacher became a part of it.

In the following years Doddy became an evangelist greatly used by the Lord. His calling was first to his own Javanese people. Using a van, he led a team that showed the Jesus film in villages. He used familiar stories to illustrate God's truth. Many Muslims came to faith. Invitations came from churches all over Java. Later he was invited to other islands and led powerful evangelistic outreaches leading many to Jesus.

As his ministry grew God opened doors abroad, even to Canada. He was invited to be part of Billy Graham's Conference of Evangelists held in Amsterdam in 1983. Three years later my wife Melita and I were privileged to attend the Billy Graham sponsored Amsterdam 1986 Congress of Evangelism. Doddy had proposed our names. God is indeed a God of miracles.

She said, "I Believe"

Anonymous in Asia, 2018

It's not often that cross cultural friendships begin easily, but this one did. Rosie was kind and generous with my language mistakes, and she knew a bit of English to fill in the gaps. We laughed together and she played sweetly with my baby. She was lovely. That first day in the park, we exchanged numbers.

I wasn't expecting to meet again—as life in a large city makes connections challenging—but meeting with Rosie came naturally. She was of the minority people in the area. She lived alone in a dorm, her family was out in the village, and she was in the city studying. We enjoyed leisurely afternoons drinking tea while my baby napped, or would go out for walks in the morning, with my baby in the stroller. We would go to cafes and study words together; I would help her with her studies and she with mine. She knew from our second meeting that I was a Christian, and yet she persisted in friendship. She was a Muslim.

Rosie had many spiritual questions for me, and one day she read the book of John in her own language in our apartment. That night she got a call from her dad in the village. Her brother had been arrested in the city and sent to a camp. She needed to return to the village immediately, to remain safe, he said. She left our apartment with a wildly fearful look in her eyes. Would we see one another again? In those days one could never be sure.

Shortly after, Rosie invited my husband and I to come out to her village which was risky, but her village was a tourist area so we figured our visit would be justifiable in the eyes of the government. We enjoyed two days together. One day was at her parent's home where she took me into a side room where we could talk alone. I gave her a children's storybook Bible with a few little notes in it. "These are the rest of the stories you were reading at my house," I told her. Rosy was pleased. She wrapped the book back up. In the following weeks and months, we would message back and forth. I would send her a photo of the page I suggested she read, and a little encouragement to let her know I was praying for her. She would reciprocate, sending the corner of a page and thoughts she was having. These check-ins were precious and I know the Spirit was at work in her.

Toward the end of our stay in that area I made a quick train trip to visit her one more time. We had a chaperone-type person with us on almost the entire visit and there was surveillance technology almost everywhere. Personal conversation was challenging. I mentioned to her in a brief moment alone with her, that I could give her a phone chip with the rest of the Bible and some other Christian materials on it. Did she want it? In another moment alone she whispered, "Yes, I want it."

We were driven to the train station, and she walked me to the train platform. There were cameras everywhere, but this was a better place than in the car with the chaperone. I pulled the phone chip out of its hiding place. As we reached down to zip up the bag together, I slipped the chip into her hand and she tucked it away. We hugged a big hug because we were sure we'd never see each other again. A week later I got a message: She said, "I believe." Oh, how I would love to know what that statement meant and what it means to her now. Will I see her again? This is the hardest part of this line of work: leaving loved ones behind.

Opportunity Knocks

Linda Nagel in Côte d'Ivoire, 1986

Occasionally, our visit to a village coincided with another event and seemed inopportune, but God would turn these times around and make them a blessing. Such was the time we arrived in Woro.

"We're just about to make a big sacrifice," the chief said. "If you want to wait you can." Of course we would wait. We didn't want to miss an opportunity to share the gospel or to witness the customs of the people.

A big ram was tied to a pole ready for slaughter. Soon the Imam, the religious leader, arrived. A crowd of men gathered around the ram as it was led into the circle. They placed their hands on the head of the animal. Those who couldn't get near put their hands on the shoulders of those who could. Then the Imam pronounced their requests to Allah. The men all bowed their heads and covered their eyes with their free hand as he spoke, "May this sacrifice bring rain, bountiful crops, wealth, protection from our enemies, peace in our village and freedom from illness..." and much more.

Everyone responded to the blessings as they were given with Ameena (amen). The ram was then thrown on the ground and someone with a sharp knife cut its throat. Blood gushed out on the ground and the men began cutting off the skin and dividing the meat into portions, one for each family represented. They passed the meat along to their wives. Then the women handed everyone a piece of sweet rice cake as part of the ritual.

Soon the ceremony was over and the chief turned to us. "Now you can speak," he said.

Helen Krueger loved a challenge and I believe an anointing came on her from the Lord. While the dogs licked up the blood on the ground Helen began to preach. "You've covered almost everything with the prayer made at this sacrifice," she stated, "but you didn't ask for the forgiveness of sins."

"Oh no," said the chief. "This sacrifice cannot cover the forgiveness of sin."

"Well, let me tell you about one that will."

They were all ears. Even the women, who were trying to cook the meat and prepare a feast, did not want to miss what was being said. Helen told of creation, the first sin, man's disobedience to God and how a sacrifice was required to cover their sin. All through man's early journey they made a sacrifice to regain a relationship with God but the Bible says the blood of bulls and goats is not enough.

The story was long, but the Barala love stories and as Helen spoke the chief responded with nama—a word to say, yes, we're following. Then she came to the part where God himself gave a sacrifice that met the requirement of the law, a just man dying in the place of mankind.

"When you sacrificed the ram, you divided it up and every family had to partake for the sacrifice to be effective. In the same way every individual must accept that Jesus died, for them to be forgiven and have eternal life."

Deep silence. My heart was bursting with prayer that they would see the truth, believe in the Lord Jesus Christ and be saved.

Beyond the Mud *(2015) by Linda Nagel, page 130.*

Saved through Revelation

Walter Mohr in Indonesia, 1964

"Then I saw another angel flying in mid-air, and he had the eternal gospel to proclaim to those who live on earth – to every nation, tribe, language and people. He said in a loud voice, 'Fear God and give him glory, because the hour of his judgment has come. Worship him who made the heavens, the earth, the sea and the springs of water." Revelation 14:6-7

When we rented the house in Madiun across from Radjum's home we were not welcomed enthusiastically. We sensed distrust and the unspoken question, "What are these white faces doing here?" Our coming renewed memories of a dark colonial past. Along with other neighbours, Radjum offered us uneasy smiles and polite greetings. However, we learned later, that beneath those smiles lurked dark suspicions and even sinister schemes. Along with other neighbours, he was convinced that my morning routine was far from harmless. I would sit on my front steps (to get better reception) and pull out the aerial of my transistor radio to listen to the BBC news. He was suspecting that I was really connecting with CIA. I was probably a dangerous foreign agent.

But now six months later, Radjum was reading the Bible. In our first conversations he defended his faith vigorously. How arrogant to say that Jesus was the Son of God and the only way of salvation? Although he was not an observant Muslim, he was loyal to the prophet from Mecca. If there was only one way, Islam was the way. But an inner hunger drew him to visit again and again. I sensed that he was a truth-seeker. Repeatedly I shared the good news called the Injil. I explained it with verses from the Bible and using large flip-charts. He was listening more and arguing less.

Then he bought a Bible. I forgot to make my usual suggestion. Begin reading at Luke or John's Gospel. So, he had flipped through the big volume wondering where to start. He found the index—the names were strange and meaningless but the final one, Wahyu sounded interesting. It meant something revealed. "Ah," he concluded, "perhaps it reveals something to me?" And it did.

Backing up a bit. Radjum was not a model citizen. He was nursing a lot of anger. His family had given him away to live with an uncle and aunt who had no children. He resented his siblings and parents. He felt rejected. He developed coping skills but was haunted by questions: Why am I living here? Why was I given away? Why was I even born? Why did I have no playmates?

And, he found playmates—the wrong kind. He was now known to police. Although he was still a teenager he had been in trouble with the law. He was a member of the blue jean gang. At this stage the crimes were not major but did disturb the peace in the neighbourhood. He had learned to be tough. He questioned everything. He needed to prove himself.

He found the book of Revelation weird but also engaging. Such strange symbolism—voice like a trumpet, a sea of glass, four strange creatures around a throne, a scroll no one dared open, trumpet blasts, a red dragon, beasts with horns, a star falling from the sky, angels flying through the air. It just didn't make sense. He visited a few times to complain and express his doubts about this strange book which was called the Holy Bible. But he kept reading.

Then he came to 14:6 and that word *Injil* (gospel) caught his attention. He read and reread that verse. Was this somehow relevant to him now? He came to our house with questions. "Is this the same Injil that you keep talking about?" My answer was simple. "Of course it is. After all it is called the eternal Injil—there is only one eternal Injil—foreshadowed in the Garden of Eden and fulfilled in Jesus Christ; only one good news story and it is about

God's love as revealed in Jesus and his death on the cross for us sinners. This good news is for every tribe, language and people." He pondered that a bit but did not argue. Then his second question, "Is it true what this verse says about the hour of judgment?"

"Yes," I said. "That is also true. And that is why the angel's message is a call to give God glory and worship Him." His defences were down and he was trying to comprehend the implication.

Then came the big question, "How can I make this good news my experience?" Together we bowed the knee to Jesus and prayed. Radjum, a confessing sinner, invited Jesus to be his Saviour and Lord. And Jesus changed everything. I had long known that John 14:6 was special. That day Revelation 14:6-7 also became special.

The change was so evident that within a short time he brought a message from his adopted parents. They were sending their thanks and gratitude for changing their son's life. Of course, they were thanking the wrong person. God, working by his Spirit through his word had done that. I was simply the neighbour God sent to live across the street.

Then Radjum came requesting tracts. He wanted others to know this good news. He asked for tracts that pictured hell fire. I did have some tracts that had fire pictured on the top of the first page. Boldly he handed them to his school friends as well as to teachers at his high school. Some listened and came to visit us; others became angry. He lost many friends. His zeal was amazing, as was his spiritual growth. Soon he was joining me in evangelistic outreaches to villages around Madiun. He became an effective evangelist and then a pastor. Eventually most of his own siblings—who had considered him the black sheep in the family, became Christians. He showed wisdom and faithfulness. Some years later the emerging denomination of ex-Muslims chose him to be the general superintendent.

Thirty years later when Melita and I were visiting Indonesia again, Radjum and Purwati his wife came to visit. They posed a sobering question. "What would have happened to us if you had not rented that small house across the street from us? I was on a path of certain destruction. Thank you for coming." Melita and I could only answer, "God sent us, He alone deserves the glory." And indeed, He does.

The Nanny

Anonymous in Asia, 2017

When we returned to Asia with our newborn baby we moved into a flat and quickly realized the need for a nanny. A friend gave us a recommendation; a 65-year-old woman with experience working for expat families. We interviewed her and loved her demeanour. She didn't speak English at all which was a major benefit for my language development. We enjoyed our afternoons together. I could study at home or go to meet my tutors, while she aptly took care of my baby. While he slept, we sometimes cleaned the apartment together, chattering all the while. She would sing and talk to my baby in the foreign language. We loved being good employers to her, offering her raises, and paid holidays. She loved working for us and we wanted to keep it that way. She was our most trusted helper, and yet she wasn't a believer.

We needed to keep some key elements of our life hidden to avoid being turned-in to the authorities. At this time the government was incentivizing citizens to report any and all religious activity, so we had to hold our cards close. She knew we were Christians. My husband and I prayed often for God to be our guard. We could only do so much to stay safe and continue to do the work without being paralyzed by fear.

We kept our contraband literature in the cereal cupboard. Our cereal cupboard contained boxes of real cereal intermingled with cereal boxes filled with New Testament literature in banned languages. One day when I reached for the cereal, I realized that our nanny had kindly rearranged the boxes: literature boxes on the left, cereal boxes on the right.

Conversations with the nanny went deeper, and we knew more about her family and she knew more about ours as the months went by and our baby grew taller. She adored our son and we thanked God for sending her to us, but we wanted her to get more out of this situation than just employment; we wanted her to find relationship and forgiveness in Christ. One day I asked her how many foreign families she'd served; 36 other families, many of them had been Christians. "What is stopping you from also being a Christian?" I asked her directly.

"I want to be in charge of my life," she said, her eyes brimming with tears. We talked about that a bit more, then put the faith conversation back on the shelf to be dusted off another day.

When we eventually had to leave the country, we gave her some of our best possessions. She was grateful especially for the beautiful duvets as the cold winter approached. We trusted that consistent acts of kindness partnered with direct and honest presentations of truth would sow seeds in her heart. A year later we heard that she had been diagnosed with cancer. The fear of death pushed her beyond her desire to "control her own life." She came to faith then quickly, on her own, as she had heard so much about Jesus over the years. Then the report was that her children also came to faith that same year, in separate locations and without each other's knowledge. God had orchestrated salvation for the family and they were overjoyed to find out they would all be citizens of a far better kingdom someday.

Treasure in the Garbage Can

Walter Mohr in Indonesia, 2008-9

He felt guilty doing it. It was not his business to poke around in other people's garbage cans. And the letter was not addressed to him. But no one was looking so he quickly picked it up. Dwi was a labourer churning a cement mixer. He was part of a crew doing a renovation project in a Muslim home in Java.

The stamp caught his eye. From Canada? Perhaps there is money in the envelope? He took a quick look inside and was disappointed. It only contained several pieces of paper. He was about to throw it back into the garbage when a voice within seemed to say, "Put it in your pocket. It might be for you."

That evening, when finally alone he read and reread the letter and tract. The letter mentioned an offer of a free correspondence course to learn about Jesus. It mentioned that Jesus the Messiah was mentioned many times in the Koran. Would he like to know more? Soon tears were flowing down his cheeks and he was hiding from his wife lest she sees him weeping and thinks of him as a sissy.

A few weeks later I was opening a letter that arrived at our post office box in Hamilton, Ontario. The following are some excerpts. "My friend from Canada, your letter from a far country was sent to this village to this city to this address—to a place of great need. The words in that tract haunt me. My friend, my religion is Islam. But I am drawn to your course. The tract said that it was sent to you. I picked it up. I took it home. I believe it was sent for me. It also said that it was sent to you, a sinful person. That definitely applies to me. My brother, please help me. Guide me to the path of light and away from the darkness that I feel within me."

A letter of welcome along with lesson number one was soon in the mail to Dwi. Reading verses from the Koran as well as verses from the Bible he learned that Jesus was much more than a prophet. He learned truths found in the Koran he had never heard before. That Jesus was the only sinless prophet. That he was the only virgin-born prophet. That he was the only prophet who raised the dead. And that Jesus was the only prophet already in heaven. He was astounded.

Dwi also learned that it was Jesus' love for sinners that led Jesus to the cross to die for people just like him. Only a few years ago Dwi was hailed a hero. He had led a young Christian girl to renounce Christ and become a Muslim. His arguments and her love prevailed. To him it proved that her religion was inferior and Islam was superior. Now they had two small children. As he continued his studies the sense of his unease and his sinfulness increased. The beauty of Jesus, the Saviour also increased.

His trust in Jesus was quickly taking root. A month later he wrote, "My faith has moved ahead of me, I already love Jesus Christ. Amen." He asked some difficult questions but the Holy Spirit brought conviction. His mind could not fully understand but his heart knew that Jesus was the way.

Dwi also knew that the cost of leaving Islam was high. He lived near a huge madrasah and his area was fanatical in observing the pillars of Islam. He would be shunned by his friends. He would be called an infidel. He would be mocked. He might lose his job. But increasingly he understood that Jesus is the true light and he must follow Jesus. Dwi made the right choice.

As Dwi continued his studies the tone of his letters changed. Then this note of praise came to our post office box. "Brother, a big thank you to you, and to the Lord Jesus, who chose me and my family to become his children. Once I was in darkness but now, I am in the light. Now I have a heavenly Father, Jesus Christ is my Saviour and Redeemer and the Holy Spirit is my comforter and guide."

"Brother, with joy I tell you that I have sealed my commitment to Jesus

Christ by publicly confessing the Apostle's Creed and by baptism in a local church. I was baptized on February 15th at 6 p.m. My wife was beside me. She has repented of turning her back on Christ to follow Islam. Our two young children were also baptized and we renewed our wedding vows as Christians. As a family our hearts have been renewed. God's Spirit touched us and Christ Jesus our Lord illuminated our hearts. Now I shed tears of gladness and blessedness. Thank you for mailing that envelope. I found it in a garbage can but it held great treasure."

When Jesus Opens the Door

Karli in Central Asia, 2023

Recently I took a guest from Canada to a large mosque with a lady's section. It is heart-touching to see the people doing their five-times-a-day prayer.

As we wandered around, I heard some ladies speaking the language I was learning so I called out a friendly greeting. When the ladies heard their language, they came over for a chat.

One young lady told us she would be graduating from her bachelor's program at university the next day. She was from a remote place and just visiting our city for a few days. As we chatted, she asked my young Canadian friend what she had studied. My friend had studied the Bible in school and hesitated for a moment, uncertain about sharing in that context, but then she didn't hold back. To our amazement, the lady gave her a high five and said, "That is so awesome! I have always wanted to read that book. I am looking for it. My best friend at university somehow found one in English, there were three or four of us longing to read it and said she could give it to me when she was finished trying to read it but our school year ended and she never gave it to me. I am still longing to read that book. My family will be very upset with me but if I ever find it, I am still going to read it." Wow. Our Father had answered our prayer and put hunger in the hearts of these young female students.

How delighted she was when I showed her a Bible app in her own language.

The door was wide open for a long chat about our Redeemer.

VII

Discipling

Train up a child in the way he should go and he will not depart from it.
Proverbs 22:6

When conversions happen on the mission field, missionaries are often tasked with discipling these infants in the Lord. It is part of the follow-through. In this, the Holy Spirit has been known to do the heavy lifting. Often a new believer's spiritual senses are heightened. Their experience of conviction is extreme. They hunger for the word. Inevitably the discipled and the mentor both grow.

Breaking Bondages

Walter Mohr in Indonesia, 1971

Adji and Ate (pronounced Awe-tay) came to us with an unusual request. "There is a foul odour in our house. Can you come to pray?" We had often been invited to homes to pray, but praying that a foul smell disappears? That was a new one! My first thought was, have you checked for a dead rat? I did not ask that. These were intelligent well-educated people. There had to be something deeper.

Two years earlier Adji had accepted Christ as his Saviour. I preached from Hebrews that morning: "Jesus, the one who saves to the uttermost." I do not know what drew Adji to attend. Perhaps it was some bondage? Was there an inner hunger that he was trying to satisfy? Was some fear haunting him? Did someone invite him? Had he developed an interest in one of young ladies who were part of the congregation? Perhaps it was that last one. Whatever drew Adji, within four months of his conversion he and Ate were sitting in our home asking questions about marriage. Ate was a mature zealous Christian and a highly respected nurse midwife. She was also active in our growing Sunday school ministry. About a year later I preached at their marriage.

Adji was an artist, a photographer and university professor. He owned a lovely home and a well-equipped photography studio. Lovely large murals that he had painted graced his studio walls. Now in his late twenties he had done well and was respected in our city. He had identified as a nominal Muslim. But back to this strange request. After some questions I began to understand why they were so troubled. They suggested that the foul smell originated from some powerful charms. These were keris Adji had inherited. We knew then that we were dealing with a satanic bondage. This was spiritual warfare, a battle between darkness and light. We were facing a power encounter but could move forward in faith unafraid. Jesus often cast out evil spirits and he has given us, his followers, power over all the power of the enemy.

Though we did not fear we also knew the importance of being prudent. Satan is a strong foe. Often, he counterattacks. We suggested that we would gather some mature believers who were acquainted with such matters and come to their home later that afternoon. As a team united in Jesus' name, we would be stronger. We had to come wearing the full armour of God. In Indonesia demonic powers are very real. Such powers are sought for status, wealth, and control. Shamans often spend weeks fasting in caves or mountains to gain special demonic powers. They bring bondage and darkness into lives.

When Melita and I arrived at Adji's home he was lighting a bonfire. Soon he brought out the two valuable beautiful daggers, called keris. They had been wrapped in decorated cloth. The sheaths were artistically engraved. Keris are tools used by shamans, and Adji's father was one. They are wavy daggers crafted by men who practice sorcery and black magic. One of the daggers was about 30 centimetres long and the other was perhaps 75 centimetres long. Spiritually powerful daggers are made by blending metals while calling on the spirits to indwell the dagger. Adji told us that when his father died, he begged Adji to accept these gifts and to tend them as he instructed. That included taking them out of their protective cloth periodically and burning incense to them. Adji was familiar with evil powers and did not want these gifts but to honour his father he accepted them.

Adji was now a Christian. Since his conversion he had not tended the keris as instructed. He had stored them in a dresser drawer and ignored them. He had struggled with what to do with them. The foul odour now made this an urgent matter. He was certain that the evil smell in the house emanated from those daggers and he wanted to dispose of them and be rid of the stink.

But he needed help. People seeking spiritual powers would have paid him a handsome sum for these charms. He rightly believed that selling them would not release him from bondage and would bring others into bondage. So, he was taking the step he saw other believers in our young fellowship take. It was also what he read had happened in Ephesus as recorded in Acts 19:17-19 where costly fetishes were burned.

Then Adji confessed to a further bondage. Before becoming a Christian, he had planted a white bamboo in front of his house. In Java it is commonly believed that evil spirits travel through the air in straight lines. His house stood directly at the head of a dead-end street. This meant evil spirits would have easy and direct access to his house. To prevent that, he had been told (perhaps by his father) that he needed to plant a white bamboo in front of the house. This would confuse the spirits and they would not enter his house. "Now," he said, "I am trusting in Jesus for protection and not a white bamboo. So, I publicly declare that this bamboo is powerless and chop it down and burn it in Jesus' name."

As a team we were thrilled hearing his testimony, seeing his spiritual insights and courage. We rejoiced that he was addressing this matter seriously and taking drastic measures. Drawing on previous experiences we guided Adji with specific steps in this spiritual cleansing. We could not do this for him. They were his charms, and had become his burden. Only he could properly deal with them. As we worshipped God, Adji should show his disdain for the keris. We suggested that he bend and break them in Jesus' name. He should then throw them into the fire along with the bamboo he had cut down. As he was doing this, he should publicly renounce the devil and all his works in the name of Jesus.

Adji did all the above as neighbours watched from a distance. Adji and Ate then joined the circle of believers around the flames and smouldering embers. We sang praises to God, prayed and quoted scripture verses reminding the devil that he is a defeated foe, and that Jesus in us is greater than the satanic powers in these sacred objects. In our prayers we thanked the Father that Jesus gave his children authority over the powers of darkness. It was a powerful testimony to neighbours who were watching and strengthened the faith of all of us who participated.

It was a glorious afternoon of celebration. Adji and Ate never again spoke of a foul odour filling the house. Jesus had triumphed. Adji and Ate continued to serve Jesus faithfully. They carried a special burden for those in our city prison. They regularly visited and preached in the prison. Bondages had been broken in their lives and in their home and they wanted to see others released from Satan's grip. Jesus came to set the prisoner free. And he is still doing it.

Alejandro's Story

Karen Morris in Spain, 2022

I first met Alejandro when he was six years old. He fondly remembers beating me at chess the first time his parents had me over for a meal. His older brother, Juan, was in grade nine at the time and coming to the after-school homework classes at the church. Juan started coming to the teen outreach, then the church's youth group, and then he accepted Jesus in 2014 and was baptized in 2015. From the start, he would bring his two younger brothers, Alejandro and José, to the Saturday kids clubs and vacation Bible school each summer where for years they heard the stories of Jesus and learned the Bible verses. In 2017, Alejandro and his family moved from the town of Torrejón to the small town of Cabanillas about a half hour's drive away.

Juan went through a difficult time when he started dating a non-Christian and drifted away from the church, but he called me when Alejandro, now in grade seven, was failing math. For the next three months until school finished, I would drive to their house every other Sunday to have lunch and study with Alejandro. Often, it was Alejandro himself who made lunch as he wants to be a chef and open his own restaurant one day.

Education is highly valued by Alejandro's parents, Rodrigo and Julia, who both finished university in Bolivia before immigrating to Spain. This caused a lot of conflict between Juan and his father, and Alejandro and his father over grades and furthering their education. However, it also made Rodrigo and Julia very grateful for the support I was able to give their sons. They often invited me over for a meal or to stay the weekend after they had moved to Cabanillas, which allowed for very interesting conversations about God. They had both been raised Catholic but Rodrigo especially is closed to God and religion. For a year and a half, Alejandro would take a bus and then a train to study at the homework classes at the church. In the fall of 2019, he started staying after class for the youth meetings at the church and he gave his life to Jesus in November 2019. We continued studying online during the pandemic and lockdown but would often spend more time talking about Jesus and the Bible than his homework.

After the pandemic, a new church was planted in his small town and he started to attend, and is being discipled. He was baptized in July 2022. It was a special day with his whole family in attendance. He gave his testimony standing in the cold waters of the river Tajo where he bravely asked his father's forgiveness saying, "I'm sorry for the things I did and said and for everything I made you suffer, even to the point of not wanting to call you, my father. I'm sorry and I love you, but not as much as my heavenly Father loves you. I hope one day that you are here with me in the church and that one day, we can meet up in heaven and worship God together." It was powerful to see this hardened Bolivian father in tears. We continue to pray for this precious family; for the salvation of Rodrigo, Julia and José; for Juan to return wholeheartedly to Jesus, and for Alejandro's continued growth in the Lord.

Joseph finds the Truth

Linda Nagel in Côte d'Ivoire, 1980's

Joseph, came to church when he could. He had attended my classes in primary school and was now in high school in another town. Summer holidays in the village gave him opportunity to borrow books from our library. He told us he had precious memories of when we taught him the Bible stories at school and would like to buy a Bible. Along with the Bible, we gave Joseph a cassette tape containing the testimony of a converted Muslim imam.

Joseph returned radiant, "This is the truth. I know it. What really spoke to me was the verse I learned when I was in your classes."

"And what verse was that?" I asked.

"Jesus said, I am the way, the truth and the life. No one comes to the father but by me."

A few weeks later Joseph experienced further spiritual revelations. "Even before you came to Boko," Joseph explained, "I knew there was something wrong with Islam. Why should one have to pay to be approved by God? In Islam, to be saved, you have to pay to go to Mecca, pay alms to the poor, give gifts to the imam, all to gain favour. In other words, the poor can never be saved. When you came and told us that God made salvation a free gift for everyone that really spoke to me."

Shortly after this, Joseph returned to San Pedro to attend school. The seed, firmly sown, was taking root and I prayed that Joseph would return to Boko someday and lead others to the truth. God was adding to his church and what a privilege to partner with God.

Beyond the Mud *(2015) by Linda Nagel, page 173.*

More Than a Chance Encounter

Amy in the Middle East, 2015

One of our workers, Amy helps lead a ministry training program. Her group of ministry students never knew what to expect when they went out on their regular visits to the local bus station to bring food to the homeless and to find people to pray for and bless.

One evening they noticed a family sitting together, looking lost. "Where are you going?" enquired the students. This family was fleeing from danger in their home country and had only just arrived, they were figuring out their next steps. The students gladly showed them where the UN offices for refugees were located and helped with their other questions. Then Amy asked if they had a place to stay, her heart quickened at the response. "We have nowhere to go, do you know of somewhere cheap we can stay until our UN interview in a few weeks." Amy had just changed apartments yet had paid the rent in her old place for a few more weeks. She took a risk and invited the family of ten to use her old place until they could find another temporary place to stay while their papers were processed.

What a relief for this family, whose home had been ravaged by years of war and now by the presence of terrorists. Before their long and difficult journey, the sons spent nights guarding their village from attacks. After terrorists shot their uncle, they decided it was time to flee.

Thousands of refugees have poured into this country causing tension among local people. Amy was met with anger by her neighbours for bringing a foreign family inside, but she sought to bring peace, and in answer to much prayer, the family stayed on.

One evening, over tea together, the conversation naturally led to Amy sharing the gospel story. The man with the best English translated faithfully for his family as she shared the simple story of a loving God. When she shared what God did in coming to earth and dying on the cross, he hesitated with emotion.

The following day the family was given a copy of the Jesus film. When the man who had translated realized it was the same story from the night before, he received it with joy.

God continued to meet with this family in the following months. One of the brothers suffered from pain in his stomach. Amy and the students prayed for him. He was healed. On another evening Amy's friend prayed for the mother who hadn't been able to sleep for days. She slept well that night and thereafter. One sister struggled with a dark heaviness and was ill and depressed, but when Amy's friends prayed, the darkness lifted and this woman heard a voice saying, "Do not be afraid. I'm caring for you."

Amy says, "While we have laughed a lot with this family, we also sat and cried with them the night the terrorists invaded their hometown, killing, capturing and forcing others to flee to the mountains without food or water." The family asked her and others to pray for their remaining relatives. They learned later that a grandmother they assumed had died on the mountain, had actually been rescued, and an uncle and sister who were captured were eventually miraculously released.

One of the brothers who was greatly affected by the gospel message, was asked if he would like prayer to meet Jesus for himself. He and his wife welcomed the prayer. The following day he felt awful and didn't know how to shake the feeling. He tried playing games and laughing with his family, but the awful feeling persisted. Unable to sleep, finally he said, "Okay Jesus, If you are who they say you are, I need you to come and help me." Then he heard a sound at the window. He looked up, didn't see anything, but heard a voice telling him to drink some water. As he drank, the bad feeling completely lifted. With excitement he told his wife, "Jesus is here. Jesus is here." She smiled and suggested that he then pray for her side which had been hurting her all day. He did, and she was healed! She later saw Jesus in a dream. Still later, when Amy and the students pointed out the story of Jesus speaking to the Samaritan woman about living water, he declared, "that's what I drank that night!"

About three months later, some of the family had visas to continue the immigration process, but others were rejected despite repeated attempts.

The brother and his wife, who had the Jesus encounters, remained in the same town with Amy and her community where they would meet regularly for Bible study. After some time they stated, "We want to follow Jesus now." Amy was surprised since she had understood that they were already believers, so she asked what they meant. They replied, "up to now we believed in Jesus, but now we want to take the step of following him. We want to be baptized."

Update from Amy, 2024: This family was baptized and subsequently joined the ministry school before finally receiving acceptance to the United States as refugees where they were reunited with family members.

VIII

First Things First

Night and day, whether he (the farmer) sleeps or gets up, the seed sprouts and grows, though he does not know how. All by itself the soil produces grain—first the stalk, then the head, then the full kernel in the head. As soon as the grain is ripe, he puts the sickle to it, because the harvest has come."
Mark 4:27-29

Where does one start when bringing Jesus to the unreached? A first contact, a first convert, a first co-worker, a first class to teach; these are all milestones to celebrate on the road to the harvest. These milestones inject hope into what can seem like a daunting undertaking.

Co-Workers

Anonymous in Asia, 2016

We moved to Asia bright eyed and bushy tailed—a young couple who loved Jesus with our whole hearts. We definitely had no idea of the territory ahead of us, but we knew that the Lord would lead us through anything because of what he had done for us in the past. The morning after we landed, we started our first day of language class at the university. The language immersion was a shock to the system; we stood in the cafeteria line and mimicked the order of the man ahead of us. We didn't know how to count the currency, so we trustingly handed over a mitt-full of cash hoping the cashier would pass back the proper change. We walked to our table with unrecognizable food on our plates and uncountable money in our palms. We felt alone and terrifyingly inexperienced.

With full bellies, jet-lagged bodies and passionate hearts we set out for our first day of school. All students had to complete a comprehensive health examination at the traveller hospital, so we loaded into a bus and set off through the busy city of four million. The teacher gave us small booklets with various pages, akin to a scavenger hunt list, however each page meant a different health test in a different room. The X-Rays in the X-Ray room, the blood tests in the Phlebotomy room, and so on. After eight rooms the only one left on our list was surgery. This must be where they harvest organs, we joked to each other under our breath. But what on earth could surgery be? As we lingered outside the surgery room we clearly heard in perfect Canadian

English, "Here it is, the surgery room." We turned around and saw only Asians. Were we imagining this? They spoke again and we turned back to see an Asian couple, a bit older than us, speaking our same accent of English. We were called into the surgery room, and were relieved when they only took our height and weight. We left the hospital totally intact.

The next day at school we saw the same English-speaking couple; they were classmates. We introduced ourselves and found out we are from the same area in Canada. We aren't sure who was more surprised. They thought we were Russians. Through a series of cloaked conversations over the next couple of weeks we figured out that we were both here for the same reasons. We realized that God had set us up to be in that class for each other, as secret teammates, dear friends and confidantes through what would become one of the hardest seasons of our lives in unimaginable circumstances.

The next day another Asian woman, again, speaking impeccable Canadian English knocked on our dormitory door. She introduced herself and invited us to come across the hall to their room for pomelo. We didn't know what that even meant. It turned out, her and her husband were young newlyweds like us. They had heard us talking in the hallway and realized we weren't Russians (as they had also assumed) and wanted to make our acquaintance. Again, through cloaked and sensitively curious conversation, as her husband meticulously peeled the pomelo—which we were happy to realize was a fruit—we recognized we were all believers in Jesus. The sense of fellowship was instantaneous.

Between these two couples, we felt the Lord had prepared a table for us in the presence of our enemies. He had made fellowship and given us strength in numbers. The harvest is indeed ripe, and the workers are definitely few, but we were so grateful that God had connected us and sent us into the field at the same time. The next two years of ministry under a militaristic regime made these strategic friendships an irreplaceable gift from God.

First Barala Convert

Linda Nagel in Côte d'Ivoire, 1981

Gramma had a happy outlook on life and was adored by her children, but physically she wasn't strong. One morning one of her grandchildren raced over to our home with an urgent message, "Ma is very sick. Come quickly." We locked our doors, jumped into the car and drove over to her hut. She seemed to be having a heart attack and was finding it hard to breathe, so we took her to the dispensary. It wasn't quite the same as calling 911. There was no doctor at the dispensary, the nurse was out of town, and no medicine available. But there was a proper bed. Jean and I were the emergency team.

The dispensary was equipped with beds to accommodate very ill patients overnight. Family members usually took care of their sick, staying with them as long as needed. Gramma's sons helped her onto a bed. The whole family gathered around expecting the worst. Jean provided medicine from her own limited supply, and we asked the family if we could pray for her in Jesus' name. They all nodded in agreement, following their mother's feeble sign of approval and all said, "Ameena" (Amen) at the end of the prayer. We couldn't do much more, so after a while we went home.

An hour later Karamogo, Gramma's youngest son, arrived at our door. "Ma is better and wants to go home," he announced. We got in the car and drove the two hundred metres to the dispensary to pick her up. She was sitting under a tree breathing normally. Jean said it was impossible for the medicine to regulate her heart so soon. The next morning, we visited her at home and all she could say was, "Jesus healed me. Jesus healed me."

Gramma had heard the gospel over and over through the cassettes we played in the evenings and she had listened attentively to the African evangelists who help us in evangelism.

Then, one afternoon in 1981 Gramma came to our house and sat down as usual on the settee in the living room, "I haven't come for medicine today," she announced. "I want to become a Jesus person and know my sins are forgiven." We talked with her again and I prayed before asking her to pray, but she interrupted my prayer. "Tell him my name is Makoné Diomandé. I want him to know my name," she said. What a delight not only for our ears, but also for the angels in heaven who, the Bible says, rejoice over one soul who comes to Jesus! We assured her that God knew her name and wrote it on the palm of his hand. She was ecstatic. Gramma was the first Barala convert.

Beyond the Mud *(2015) by Linda Nagel, page 85-6.*

First Women's Conference

Linda Nagel in Côte d'Ivoire, 1969

Two years into my first term in Africa, my colleagues and I talked about the need for a women's retreat. African women carry a heavy load, both physically and emotionally. Providing a time apart from daily work to learn to read and receive Bible stories geared just for them would show they had value, as well as give them a time for rest.

In 1969, a WEC couple, John and Del Gunningham, moved to Oumé. They had served formerly in Belgian Congo but because of the instability of the country they could not go back with their four small children. Del had a vision to work with the women and was eager to help Marjorie and me plan and run the first women's conference. We decided to hold it at our house at Tiegba.

First, we had to convince the husbands to let their wives attend. "But who will carry our water and cook our food?" they questioned. Women's work and men's work were well defined in rural Africa. They considered it shameful for a man to carry the wood and water. We told them how much they would benefit from wives who knew how to read and better care for their families. Although not completely convinced, several of the men in the church agreed. Twenty-three women came to that first week-long conference. Being used to sleeping on woven mats at home it wasn't too difficult for the women with their nursing babies to sleep on mats on our floors. They filled the guest room, the office and living room, and since more kept arriving we rearranged our storage room to accommodate them.

After much chatter, the women and babies settled down for the night. Peace didn't last more than an hour when I heard shuffling and muttering in the living room. "What's wrong?" I asked poking my head out of my bedroom door. "Lice," was the agitated reply. "We're covered with lice."

My colleagues awakened as well. "Where did the lice come from?" we were all asking and then I remembered a hen had been nesting in the flower bed outside the living room window. She must have vacated her nest that day. Looking for new bodies to feed on, the lice had poured over the windowsill into our house. We didn't have screens, although the tiny creatures would probably slip through screens anyway.

Amidst all the jumping, scratching and crying babies there was laughter. Water was fetched to wash bodies and insecticide was liberally sprayed in the house and out. With windows wide open it didn't take too long to clear the air again and the women went back to sleep.

Despite a traumatic beginning, what fun these women had. It was probably their first holiday. The happy chatter around the cooking pots convinced the men, who occasionally stopped by to check and see if all was well, that everything was okay. The negative comment previously made by one of the men was diffused. "They'll do nothing but argue," he had said.

My colleagues gave me the job of talking about hygiene and keeping healthy. This was a great project for me because it caused me to observe more closely the preparation and care of food in the villages. An African kitchen didn't consist of much more than a lean-to made of bamboo with three stones on the ground to hold the cooking pot. What I observed caused a bit of concern to me. The pestle for pounding food lay in the dust while the mortar, where so much food was prepared stood upright when not in use. Chickens hopped in to peck any leftover scraps they could find, and goats jumped in and out at their pleasure. Dishes and utensils, though few, were sitting around on the ground uncovered, along with the cooking pots. Since the yard where the cooking takes place is completely free of grass, dust, animal dirt and baby urine were all part of the mix.

I had to somehow convince the women that most illness could be avoided just by making sure the kitchen utensils were clean and food was covered.

Flies carry disease. I drew pictures and pasted them on flannel to stick on the flannelgraph board; a dish of banana futu (pounded plantain) without a lid; a picture of a little baby defecating close to food preparation—a common sight. My flannelgraph fly sat in the child waste and then flew to the futu. Right away they saw what was happening and grimaced in horror. Flies were so plentiful they were almost ignored. The women had never considered what they carried in their little hairy legs.

I was presumptuous enough to draw an ideal kitchen for them. Today we would figure it all out on a computer, but this was before computers and I wasn't drawing a western kitchen. My picture showed a tidy outside hangar or lean-to, not much different than what they already had, but with a few simple changes. I drew a plank shelf where the dishes could be stored upside down out of reach of animals. The pestle hung on two nails on the wall. A low wooden platform provided a place for the mortars to sit upside down. Cooking pots, when not in use were also turned upside down on the platform to get them up off the ground. Basins for carrying the water used in cooking and bathing babies were hung on another nail. A simple table held a plate of food—covered, and cutlery kept in a plastic dish. A few simple changes could make a huge difference.

"Can I show this picture to my husband?" one of the women asked. "He needs to make me a kitchen like that."

We gave classes on the way of salvation, Bible women, reading, sewing and problems unique to women.

What a joy on the last evening to hear their testimonies. One woman who had never had the courage before to testify told how she saw how important it was to raise her children to know the Lord. "I want to be a testimony in my village," she said. They were all happy they had stayed the full week. On the last Sunday we all walked the two kilometres to the church singing as we went. Up to that time women's participation in the church services had been almost nonexistent, but during the service, two women prayed, two shared about two Bible women they heard about, and they all quoted verses they had memorized. We were so proud of them and by the looks on their husband's faces they were too.

We saw the results when we visited their homes. There was a new confidence in their faith and joy in knowing their lives had purpose. I also noticed the efforts they made to improve cleanliness in the kitchen. The following year we didn't have to beg women to come to conference. They were eager to participate again. Several years later the women from our WEC churches organized their own conferences and became a strong movement to support the church. A conference just for women proved to be of greater impact than we could have imagined.

Just to be Clay *(2021) by Linda Nagel, page 69-72.*

First, We Learn the Alphabet

Edith Frank (Span) in Thailand, 1990

During language studies in Thailand, I was given a Thai name, as Edith was somewhat difficult to pronounce. The name, Maytaa was chosen, which in Thai, means mercy. That's what I needed: mercy. In the morning, we would walk to the language school, and each student would sit with one of the Thai teachers. These kind and patient teachers were truly a gift from God. Not only did they teach us the Thai language, but in the course of time they would share details about their lives and the Thai culture.

For three hours, my teacher would say words and phrases in Thai, and I would try to repeat them. In Thai, words that make up a phrase are all joined together without any spacing and the language has five different tones. I found myself naturally moving my finger or hand under the table along with these tones. More than once, I saw my teacher stifle giggles inside her blouse at my pronunciation. I did enjoy writing out the Thai letters which look like calligraphy. At noon, we were sent home to write and to study on our own for three hours.

Back in Canada I had been used to being on the go as a visiting nurse, and this task of sitting in one place for many hours going over Thai words and simple phrases took some perseverance. With the fan blowing to ward off the mosquitoes and to provide some relief from the heat, I would sit at my desk by the open window. For a break, I would make a trip to the kitchen now and again, or play with Cleo, our Burmese cat.

After nine months of language study, I was asked to begin teaching Sunday School once a month. All week the Thai teacher worked with me on my Sunday School lesson until I had it all written out in Thai. I taped the words to the back of the three pictures which went with the lesson. It was my job to colour in the pictures as well; that was the easy part. On Sunday morning we sat on mats on the floor in Auntie Lim's tiny house near the church. I held up the pictures and read the story in Thai, as they listened attentively. In the months and years ahead, I enjoyed teaching the children at the Tak town church, or farther south in a small village church. I can still see some of their smiling faces, each one with their own unique personality.

Ready Or Not, Here I Come

Margie Knapp in The Gambia in 1979

During the preparation to serve the Lord in missions we were taught to be ready to "preach, pray or die at a moment's notice."

One morning during my language study in The Gambia the field director told me I was to give the Bible message to the patients waiting for treatment in the clinic. At this point I was stumbling over unfamiliar words and expressions and I talked with a strange accent. However, wanting to be obedient, I grabbed a set of flash cards and went to the clinic waiting hall. There were approximately 300 people waiting, mostly women, children and babies. It was a bedlam of anxious and noisy moms.

On the back of the large cards, a Bible story was written out in the predominant local language, Wolof. As I began to read in the loudest voice possible, everyone, even the babies, were quiet. This was like a miracle to me. I am not sure how much was understood as my pronunciation was certainly not the best, but the joy and confidence I had was surely from the Lord who is able to do above and beyond all that we can ask or expect.

The lesson I learned that morning was that *"he is my strength and my confidence and that I can do all things he asks me to do"* (Philippians 4:13). In the following days some women stopped me on the street and referred to the story I read that day. These wonderful African ladies were so forgiving of my bungling their language. In my years with them the lessons I learned from them more than exceeded anything I was able to impart.

While Buying a Table

Betty in Russia, 2015

I lived in a small town in rural northwest Russia for about two years, teaching English and connecting with people. One of my first connections came while buying a table. Nadia, the salesclerk, wanted to learn English, and so she and her son started coming for lessons. We became friends. At Christmas I showed them an excerpt from the Super Book DVD and Nadia told me she remembered seeing it on Russian TV when she was a girl, and it had gripped her heart. A year earlier she had suffered a severe family crisis and turned to the Lord. She started coming to our Bible-reading times and I noticed she gave the answers of a born-again believer.

God has remarkably changed her and her testimony at work is strong and clear. Last summer, her son, who is 14, came to faith and her five-year old daughter is a bundle of cheer. Sadly, her husband, is addicted to alcohol and is abusive. Healing is needed for the family. Almost every home is troubled by alcoholism.

Update from Betty in Canada, 2024: Nadia has remarried, to a pastor and since has had two more children. She is doing well and I am in touch with her and her daughter.

IX

Following His Promptings

Now an angel of the Lord said to Philip, "Go south to the road—the desert road—that goes down from Jerusalem to Gaza." So, he started out, and on his way, he met an Ethiopian eunuch ... As they traveled along the road, they came to some water and the eunuch said, "Look, here is water. What can stand in the way of my being baptized?"

Acts 8:26-27, 36

When prompted to pray for the people she had reached out to 50 years earlier Agnes Verner obeyed. When prompted to follow the God of the impossible no matter what, Walter and Melita found themselves on a rollercoaster ride to the field. When prompted to confront an angry man who was in the process of violently beating his wife, Linda Nagel bravely faced the risk. Like Philip, these missionaries knew that when the prompting comes from God, sooner or later something good for the kingdom happens.

A Word in Season

Agnes Verner in Thailand, 1970's

Fifty years ago, WEC was pioneering in the intense heat of northwest Thailand. Having completed my two-year probationary course, including language acquisition, I was assigned to a small circle of Thai homes built on stilts. These, by interpretation from the Thai language, were part of the village called Hothead which was part of the district called Dry-earth which was part of the province called Sun-bleached. WEC was indeed true to its calling to the lost and the least. Using my child evangelism approach, replete with pictures, songs and memory verses, to communicate the good news, I proceeded purposefully to tell them about Jesus whose name they had not yet heard. I had to depend on God's Holy Spirit to speak through my feeble effort.

Today I was reminded to pray for the seed sown way back then. Why today? Is the Lord awakening memories in the minds of people in their late 60's with the good news which lay dormant until now? Why should I, now a missionary to Cambodia for over 20 years, pray today for that close-knit Buddhist community in Tak town, Thailand?

While I mused this morning, I recalled my own father's testimony. As a 12-year-old boy he laboured like a grown man and expected to be treated like one. Since his own dad withheld such status from him, my father left home and roughed it like the unprincipled men of his day. A hardened, ungodly young person, my dad remembered a simple song which his third grade teacher taught the class in a one-room school in Alberta. His recollection of the words gradually conquered my father's proud spirit. *There is a green hill far away, without a city wall; where my dear Lord was crucified. He died to save us all.* Finally, after many years, these words helped point my father to his Saviour. Later still, my dad would comment about 'a word sown in season,' being God's instrument in bringing people to Christ.

Now I know why I should pray today for my first ever congregation of animistic villagers whom I talked to about Jesus so long ago. Surely the seed sown back then will take root and, even though I declared it to a group of teenagers yet, today, other WEC missionaries will reap full ears of grain from among those hearts in their 60's and 70's.

Following the God of the Impossible

Walter & Melita Mohr in Indonesia, 1961

Two-year rule: if a single person applied to WEC, it was understood that that person must plan to remain single for a minimum of two years.

"Get married? But we are not even officially engaged! And what about that two-year rule spelled out so clearly in Principles and Practice?" Those were our first thoughts when Earle and Ethel Frid, WEC Canada leaders, called us in for an interview the evening of December 16, 1960. A strange proposition was being set before us. Could we believe our ears? We were being asked to consider getting married in the next two weeks. Indeed, marriage was a dream, but from our understanding of Principles and Practice it was a distant dream. WEC's two-year rule was clear on this point. Deep in our hearts we rather disliked that rule but sensing God's call to WEC and to Indonesia we had embraced it. Of course, we did not voice our questions—we were simply stunned.

I, Walter, had joined WEC nearly two years earlier. I was an accepted worker waiting for a visa to enter Indonesia. Visas for Indonesia were rarely granted in those days but I had scattered prayer cards in faith throughout Canada. Melita had only recently filled in her application forms and had just begun her candidate training period. Indeed, getting a visa for Indonesia would take a miracle. One WEC missionary in Indonesia wrote to say, "A Red Sea lies before you but if your call is truly of God, persevere and it will happen." WEC leaders had made strong suggestions that I consider going to another field—Pakistan was open, Brazil needed workers.

Then a devastating letter came directly from the leaders of WEC Indonesia. It seemed to totally shut the door and take away all hope. The letter addressed to Earle Frid suggested that it would be best for me to forget Indonesia and seek God's direction for some other field. Hearing this news the Lord led me to embark on a three-day fast in which I asked God to clarify his will and what our next step should be. Then God again gave an amazing confirmation that it was right to expect that the door to Indonesia would somehow open. It came as we visited a church in St. Catharines. God spoke through a message given in tongues with an interpretation. The message was so unmistakably clear, "I have shown you my will, I am the God of the impossible."

"Did we love each other? Were we both committed to going to Indonesia? Could we be married here in Beamsville within the next two weeks?" We were dumbfounded and looked at each other with questioning eyes. "Yes," we nodded. "We do love each other. Yes, we are committed to Indonesia. But getting married in two weeks? Please give us time to answer that question; we need to talk to our parents."

So it was that WEC leaders actually made the marriage proposal for us. As obedient WECers we simply said, "Yes." It took a bit longer than two weeks but we were married within six weeks of that conversation. Melita's parents insisted that their youngest daughter celebrate this joyful occasion with them in Vancouver. Soon Melita was on a train heading west to help arrange wedding details. I followed a few weeks later. We were married in Vancouver on January 28th 1961. Once again visa application papers were filled in and sent to Indonesia. The second miracle came five months later via a cable sent from Indonesia, "Visa granted." Three months later we were in San Francisco preparing to embark on a 35-day cruise across the Pacific on the freighter, the SS Steel Executive, to the land of God's calling.

Fifty-two years later we still marvel at God's strange and miraculous ways. WEC has rules but WEC also shows flexibility and discerns God's best. We know they did this in our case.

Cheating Death

Walter Mohr in Indonesia, 1967

Suk was seated on the back seat of the white and blue Lambretta scooter I was driving. We were heading home with thankful hearts after a successful house-church meeting fifty kilometres from our home base. A district agriculturist had come to faith and had opened his spacious home for meetings.

Our journey home involved navigating a narrow road, half paved and half rough broken pavement and gravel. Every vehicle on the road wanted to drive on the paved area. Driving on broken pavement and gravel is especially difficult when riding a scooter. So, even though the rules of the road dictated that I drive on the left side—the rough part, I chose to drive in the middle of the road on pavement as close to the broken area as possible.

Along the way, a south wind blew the flap of my cap down to partially cover my eyes. At that moment I saw a huge dark green military vehicle speeding toward me. The huge bumper was only a few yards away. Surely the driver had seen me earlier but no horn had sounded.

I recall a sense of calm resignation. Death seemed certain! I nudged the scooter to the left onto the gravel. As I did, there was a scraping sound of metals clashing. I was able to slow the scooter to a stop. The huge truck also stopped and soldiers shouted in anger. My starter pedal had bent far back and was useless. But we were alive, shaken, but thankful. We slowly started up again and Suk blurted out, "Satan is angry."

As we limped home I pondered. What if I had not obeyed God's nudge to replace the bald tires with new ones that morning? It was the Lord's prompting. New tires with good grip may well have saved our lives. I cheated death on June 28, 1967. New tires. God's mercy. God's protection. God's nudge.

Confronting a Wife-beater

Linda Nagel in Côte d'Ivoire, 1989

I was continually learning that God is able to exchange the inadequacies of our human efforts with his strength. As Boko developed, houses were built all around us and eventually rented out to civil servants. The government transferred their personnel every two or three years so our neighbours often changed. We made friends with all of them. During one period of time, we ended up with wife-beaters on every side.

Most beatings took place in the early evenings when men came home from work, but one early afternoon terrible screams issued from the house across the road. The wife, a Muslim, was a good friend of ours and attended the French Bible study. We wondered if her husband was angry because she attended Bible study, but he had never indicated his disapproval. The screaming became more intense.

"I have to go over there," I told Jean. It was impossible to just sit and listen, but also a frightful prospect to face an angry husband. He might turn on me. I decided to take the risk and walked over to their yard. Our friend was crouched down on a stool covering her head with a cloth while her husband beat her with a whip, yelling insults at her.

He didn't see me till I asked in my most authoritative voice, "What's going on here?" The angry husband lowered his whip and slinked into the house shutting the door behind him. I urged my friend to get up and come home with me for awhile. She eased her aching body up, leaned on my arm and walked with me to a safe haven.

I don't remember her crime but to me it was inconsequential. Jean treated her outward wounds but only God could heal her inward wounds. Her husband had bouts of uncontrollable anger, she told us, which he took out on her. Toward evening she returned home.

Her husband's visit to our home the next morning surprised me. Was he coming to warn us never to interfere again? "Thank you for coming yesterday," he said, settling into a chair in our living room. "I need to tell you a story. Once there was a man and his wife who moved into a new village. The man became very angry with his wife and started to beat her. No one intervened so the man said to his wife, 'Let's leave here and go somewhere else.' So, they moved to another village. When the husband's anger erupted again and he beat his wife, no one intervened. They decided to leave that place and go somewhere else. In the third village when the man was overcome with anger and started to beat his wife, the people stepped in and stopped him. 'We'll stay here,' he said. 'These people saved me from killing my wife.'"

He continued, "That's what you did for me yesterday. We need you."

Inadequate for such situations? Certainly, but God was not. Through experiences like these I learned to follow his promptings.

Beyond the Mud *(2015) by Linda Nagel, page 138.*

The Reluctant Leader

Mick Brown in the Middle East, 2006

Our field was looking for a new leader. This happens a lot on WEC fields. Our current leaders did not feel that they should continue in their role, partly because they sensed that many workers did not share their vision of how the field should be working. As a field we started thinking, praying and chatting with each other about who the next leader might be. Typically, no one wants to be the leader. It's not what most people feel called to the mission field to do. They want to have the time and energy to do evangelism and discipleship. In these situations, we look to the Lord to solve the question, and ask the people that we think are best suited to the role to pray about it. But what happens when people start suggesting that you should be the leader? Initially we said that we didn't feel called to that role, that we think we are better suited to be supporters of the leader rather than to be the leaders. But when more people started suggesting us, and when we were struggling to think who can take on the role, then the pressure to argue it out with God mounted.

Don't get me wrong, I don't see us as being like Moses or Jeremiah, we were neither that old nor that young and the role was not that big! But I can relate to their reluctance. My discussion with God, which included talking it through with my wife, was different from the prophets' discourses, but the reluctance was probably similar. To be honest, I prefer to avoid responsibility for other people; I want to do my thing somewhat quietly in the background. I am intrinsically selfish and fearful, and those are definitely not characteristics that you want in a leader. As I confessed these things to the one that I want to be the Lord of my life, he responded with reminders of how much he has changed me thus far, and to let me know that he is the one that wants to work through me, maybe even despite me. He asked me to trust him to do that work even in and through a weak and flawed vessel. He also reminded me that I have argued that fields are better off with leaders that do not aspire to be leaders. Being reminded of my own reasoning made me cringe and laugh at the same time. Ultimately, the thing that helped us most to be willing to take on the role, was a vision of what we felt the Lord was saying about how the field should be led. We sensed a call to encourage everyone on the field to celebrate the diversity of giftings and callings that different workers had. This meant that we were not going to strive to have rigid teams and strategies, but rather we wanted people to appreciate and support others in our field that were doing things differently. As we shared this idea of a fellowship rather than a closely defined team, this concept was confirmed by others as being from the Lord.

In WEC, leaders are elected at the annual conference where unity is sought in the decision-making. By the time conference came we knew we were the only candidates and felt it was the Lord's leading even though we felt nervous and unqualified. It was good that we had that sense of confirmation because as conference started our regional leaders persuaded the departing leaders to allow their names to stand for re-election. This meant that the field members had to choose between us. This took many meetings and days to resolve, as we and the previous leaders spent many hours outside the meeting room in amicable fellowship with one another. Ultimately, we were voted in essentially because the outgoing leaders shared that they had received a vision showing that we were the people to lead the field moving forward. It was a strange start to our role as leaders, but we felt at peace because we sensed that the Lord had called us.

Wisdom from God

Linda Nagel in Côte d'Ivoire, 1978

So many people milled around the huts on market day. Add to that the gathering crowd at our hut, all demanding attention at once. I wasn't thinking of anything other than keeping order and helping Jean with the people's medical issues, when the gendarmes (national police) arrived. One of them asked to see me so I stepped outside the busy circle, found a bench and we sat down. Important business is never discussed standing up.

"We need your car," he said without hesitation. "We've been told a man in a village has been stocking up on guns and we need to catch him today. We came on a bus and don't have our own vehicle here. We'll bring it back when we're finished."

I sat for a moment wondering how in the world I should respond to a gendarme, knowing they can make life difficult if they don't get what they want. I silently called out to God for help. In the midst of the confusion around our hut there was no way I could get anywhere near Jean to ask her opinion.

God put this response into my mind: "I'm really sorry. I understand your dilemma, but as you know we have only been here a short time, and these first weeks are so important to gain the confidence of the people. We want to help them, to share the love of Jesus, to teach the Bible and bring hope to people in despair. If we start lending our car to the gendarmes we're finished. No one will trust us again and we might as well move on."

I expected an angry retort but instead the man called out to his colleagues, “Ça ne vaux pas la peine (it’s not worth it).” With that he got up and walked away.

God proved to us over and over that he cared about the big problems and the small, and he was well able to handle everything we turned over to him.

Beyond the Mud *(2015) by Linda Nagel, page 63.*

X

As Led by the Holy Spirit

May the grace of the Lord Jesus Christ, and the love of God, and the fellowship of the Holy Spirit be with you all.
2 *Corinthians* 13:14

Led by the Holy Spirit and in fellowship with him is a sweet spot. The Holy Spirit is one of the persons of God. He is all-powerful and knows everything. He convinces the unsaved of sin, of what is right, and of the judgement that happens for those who don't accept Jesus as their Saviour. At the same time, he helps the saved with power and direction and shows them how to bring the message of salvation.

When we stay in fellowship with the Holy Spirit, ultimately good things will happen. Give out one Bible at the direction of the Holy Spirit and it could lead to a Bible study with 28 men. Invite the local store owner to your Sunday fellowship and watch God grow him into a powerful, creative evangelist. Pray for healing, send out a newsletter, sit beside someone you don't know...when the Holy Spirit leads you, he'll follow through with a good result.

A Dream about a Dove

Josh in the Middle East, 2021

Andrew had received a Bible from our group three years previously and became a believer on his own. He had been waiting for someone to meet with him ever since. When one of our teammates finally did meet Andrew, they found a solid committed believer who knew his Bible well. He had been kicked out of his home and lost his job, but only became stronger in the Lord. Our team did a Bible study with him, then suggested that he teach the Bible to the people in the community.

He followed their suggestion, and the next time we visited, he brought along a friend who had had a dream about a dove. I explained the symbol of the dove in scripture. The man was relieved, because he thought Andrew had performed magic on him. They began meeting regularly to study the Bible. The next time I went, Andrew brought along another friend who had had the same dream and joined the Bible study.

Then on my next visits, I found that more men had joined the Bible study—first five guys having had the same dream, then fifteen, and now twenty-eight. They were all meeting because of this dream. Once Andrew agreed to share the Bible with his community, the Holy Spirit brought along people to join him.

The Lighthouse on Market Street

Walter Mohr in Indonesia, 1961

Born in Indonesia to Chinese parents Anwar had been given a Chinese name at birth, but after he began a serious relationship with Jesus, the light of the world, he chose a new name: Anwar—light or enlightened.

Like many Indonesians of Chinese descent Anwar, a nominal Christian, dreamed of making money and he was successful. He owned and operated Toko Baru or The New Store, a small but busy store located near the busy main market in the city of Madiun. It was our favourite grocery store in Madiun where Melita and I began our church planting career in 1961. Anwar was kind and resourceful. He sold quality goods, employed seamstresses and prepared lunches and snacks for school children. He and his wife even grew and sold orchids.

Anwar began to attend our small fellowship. His heart was touched and his life was changed. God gave him a love for Javanese Muslims. They were his faithful customers. After his conversion he immediately took steps to pattern his life on God's word. Taking a quick survey of products he was selling brought conviction. Among the most profitable products were items that made him uncomfortable. Cigarettes were top of the list. So out went all tobacco products. He filled the shelves with Bibles and Christian books. He also kept a supply of Christian tracts on the front counter visible to his customers and offered freely to anyone who showed any interest. Later when Islamic pressure made it more difficult and dangerous to openly evangelize, he found creative ways to share the gospel. One of these was to obtain newspaper-type gospel tracts and use them as wrapping paper for the goods people purchased at his store. Not everyone was thrilled at his bold witness and I am sure he lost some customers. However, he also gained a reputation as a bold Christian witness on the main business street in downtown Madiun.

As the church in Madiun grew in numbers I began to ponder the matter of New Testament church leadership. Acts 14:23 says, *"Paul and Barnabas appointed elders in each church and with prayer and fasting committed them to the Lord."* I wondered how to go about this. Knowing he was faithful and trustworthy, we had already asked Anwar to be the church treasurer. Now my mind was prayerfully searching for men who could fill the role of elders.

Anwar was a most obvious choice so I approached him with that idea. "Would you be willing to pray about being an elder if you were nominated at a church meeting?" All the people in our fellowship respected him and knew of his bold witness and leadership skills.

His answer shocked me. "Pak Mohr, I cannot be an elder. I am not an honest man." That amazed me as I knew of no one in Indonesia who was more honest than Anwar. He explained. "Every year the tax man comes to my store to collect taxes. He will ask for an exorbitant amount—a totally unfair amount. All of us business men do what is common in Indonesia. We bargain with the tax-collector and arrive at a lower compromise figure. He gets the okay from the tax office and we pay our taxes. We all know the tax initially demanded is unfair. It is how business is done and the way we survive." I remember saying, "Yes Anwar, I am sad but fully understand that we cannot ask you to be an elder." So, the matters rested.

It was about a year later one Sunday morning in 1969 when Anwar's face was beaming. It was testimony time and he hurried toward the pulpit saying he had a testimony to share. He began by saying it was a great week. The Lord had given him several messages since last Sunday but the Lord had also placed a great test before him and by God's grace, he had defeated the enemy. His story was simple. The annual tax collection time was here. As usual the tax collector had come to the store asking for an unreasonable and unfair amount of money. And as usual Anwar bargained with him and they arrived at a much lower amount. The tax man was happy saying "Anwar, get that amount we settled on ready and I will be here tomorrow morning to pick it up. I still need to get the okay from the local tax office but I am sure they will be happy with our arrangement."

Anwar could not sleep that night. He told of dreaming of that coin the Pharisees brought to Jesus when they asked Him about paying taxes. *"Give to God what belongs to God and give to Caesar what belongs to Caesar,"* Jesus had replied. Anwar spoke of that coin with that inscription continually floating before him. He could only conclude that now Jesus was speaking, not to the hypocritical Pharisees, but to Anwar the hypocrite. He got the message and knelt beside his bed promising God to pay the original amount—even if the tax was unfair and even if it meant closing his store.

The next morning the tax-collector got a big surprise. Anwar was waiting for him with that original large amount he had requested. Despite the protests of the tax collector Anwar could not be persuaded into giving less. To help keep the collector honest he insisted on a receipt for that large amount. It might be somewhat awkward for the tax-collector and also for the tax office but he felt he needed to do what was right. "Yesterday you charged me this much, and this is the amount I must give you." He then shared the reason he was doing this with the surprised tax collector. He mentioned in his testimony that he might have to charge a bit more for the bread he sold but his heart was free and rejoicing. It was a breakthrough for Anwar. When our first Madiun elders were appointed, Anwar was one of them. And praise God, Anwar's store did not end up in bankruptcy. It prospered!

Indonesian stores tend to feature portraits of famous people in a prominent place. Most often it was the nation's president and vice president. Sometimes it was family members who had founded the store. Anwar made a different choice. Behind his counter, clearly visible to every customer Anwar designed and placed four large posters printed in Indonesian. In large letters the posters in turn proclaimed: life is short, death is sure, sin the cause, and Christ the cure. Under each heading was a Bible verse confirming the truth of that bold statement. Under the last heading, John 3:16 was printed in full. Anwar's store was a lighthouse issuing a sober warning of danger ahead but also a message of eternal hope.

Anwar was called to his eternal home at age 88 in 2015. I am confident he was welcomed into Heaven with a warm handshake and a smile, *"Well done good and faithful servant. Enter into the joy of the Lord."* His youngest daughter and her husband now operate this lighthouse.

Bible Study in a Muslim Home

Derryl Bloomfield in Fiji, 2015

Soon after meeting a Muslim family in Fiji, I received a call stating the husband was in hospital for foot surgery and they wanted me to come and pray for him. This I did. The next morning, the wife called to say that God had made her husband better and the doctors had released him. When I visited their home, I asked if they wanted to know more about our God. Without hesitation they answered, "Sure, why not?"

In cases like this, we use an inductive Bible study method, relying heavily on the teaching of the Holy Spirit. We begin with creation and moved through to salvation in about twenty lessons. This family was so excited to know what the Bible says they didn't want to stop reading. They didn't have a single disagreement with us as the Bible spoke for itself.

Other Muslims approached the family to tell them not to meet with us to study the Bible but they persevered. One week, I asked a family member if he would open our Bible study in prayer. He prayed like this, "Our Father in heaven, thank you for the Bible, thank you for showing us we cannot save ourselves, thank you for Jesus Christ, thank you that he died on the cross to save us and thank you that Jesus arose from the grave three days later proving he really is God. Please help us to study your word and do whatever you tell us." The family continued to study the Bible—but they also continued to observe the Ramadan fast.

Isaiah 55:11 encourages us to depend on the leading of the Holy Spirit and share the word of God with anyone who will listen. *"My word...shall not return to me without producing an effect, but it shall accomplish that which I please and purpose, and it shall prosper in the thing for which I sent it."*

Countering The Communists

Hellen Kulesky in Liberia, 1961

Proudly proclaiming communism and that he would no longer submit to Christian teaching, a junior high schooler defied the principal and walked out of class. This provoked my righteous anger.

I had come to Liberia teaching the 3 Rs. As a Christian teacher, I hoped and prayed that my students would also come to know the truth that is Jesus Christ; but we were not winning the battle for the hearts of the young. Although WEC's Liberia Inland Mission educators had worked among the youth of Liberia for more than twenty years, we had not produced Christian firebrands like that communist student. I pondered and prayed and felt led to copy the tactics of the communists. They had used leaflets to indoctrinate the ideology of Karl Marx; we must use the printed page to indoctrinate the truth as it is in Jesus Christ.

In December, 1961, I began the first Youth leaflet with, *"Remember now thy Creator in the days of thy youth"* (Ecclesiastes 12:1a). This verse became the tagline of the leaflet. The first editions were only 100 copies and went to our Liberia Inland Mission schools. Soon other mission schools were requesting these homemade leaflets for their own use and for distribution. Not 100 copies but thousands of copies were needed. They were needed not only for Liberia but for youth around the world. Struggles with an outdated duplicating machine, leaking ink and crumpled paper often pushed me to tears and to prayer. The demand was beyond my wildest dreams. After I returned to North America the ministry expanded.

Testimonies began to reach me of lives changed and dedicated to serve Jesus: "I feel like a new person because I have accepted Jesus as my personal Saviour. I got all this news from the YOUTH papers."

"A friend told me how a copy of Youth helped change his life. I want God to control my life too."

One of my favourite testimonies is from a young Nigerian. He was on his way to a disco when someone handed him a Youth paper. He crumpled it and put it in his pocket intending to use it as toilet paper. Later, when he wanted to wash his pants, he took out the paper, read it and gave his heart and life to Jesus. His letter said he was now the president of the youth group in his church. Praise God for the power of the printed page.

Thank God for allowing me to serve him in this ministry. During the 50 years Youth was printed 9,354,240 copies of this leaflet were mailed into approximately 60 countries. Nearly 83,000 individuals wrote to us. Thanks to God for that young firebrand communist who started it all.

In Search of a Green Tree

Harry in the Middle East, 2019

We have seen many new visitors coming to our church recently and many of them have shown evidence that the Lord is working in their lives. One example is a man who recently moved here from another country in the Middle East. One night he dreamed of a green tree. He had been reading the New Testament and felt that this was somehow related.

He went on the internet in search of a green tree church. He couldn't find a church with that name, but our church has a name that starts with the same letter so he decided to visit our church. He had to travel over two hours from his part of the city to get here. When he arrived, he was surprised to see a green tree on the church sign. God led him here.

Now is the time for Africa

Cristina Grenier in Ghana, 2015

Can Africa send and support missionaries?

After 20 years of living in Equatorial Guinea the Lord called my husband Roly and I to a new exciting ministry; working with the church in Africa to mobilize our African brothers and sisters. Africa has some of the largest and fastest growing churches in the world. We could envision hundreds of missionaries going out to unreached people groups.

To accomplish our mission we moved to Ghana, a country about 30 per cent evangelical, and 70 per cent Christian. A great place to start we reasoned. We prayed and asked the Lord how to initiate this ministry of mobilizing, training, and sending African missionaries.

We began by sharing the vision with people everywhere we went, "It is the time to send African missionaries."

We cried out to the Lord, "We see beautiful churches, filled with people, but no vision to send or give support. Lord how is this going to happen?"

We searched and found a church we felt we could settle into in our new country. Soon after, a young man asked, "What do you do here in Ghana?" Roly said, "We are missionaries," to which the young man replied, "Don't you see? There is a church on every corner, we don't need missionaries here!" Roly answered, "You are right. You have so many churches, it is time you start sending people out to the unreached." The young man was taken by surprise.

Little by little we got to know the church and the people started to understand what we were doing.

One afternoon we had a knock at our door. Someone from the church had a bag of groceries for us. He said, "You are missionaries; we want to bless you."

A few weeks later, on a Sunday we shared that we were going to Burkina Faso for a ministry visit. The following Monday a young man came to our house and announced, "We want to help you with your trip up north," and he gave us an envelope. When we opened it up there was enough money to cover the fare for the bus there and back.

We needed a car and asked around about options. A Ghanaian man who imported cars said, "I am importing cars from Canada; if you know someone there, have them send a car to my company." He did not know we happened to be Canadians. We did know someone. Our friend contacted him and they arranged for the car to be delivered to the man's company.

Not long after, the Ghanaian man called us to say he was coming to our house. He arrived with our car. He had paid for all the import fees, registration and so on and just handed us the keys.

As well, a man offered us a house to live in free of charge. We had free housing for the next five years.

The Lord certainly answered the question, "Can Africans support missions?" It is not for us to question the Lord in small matters, for he says in Psalm 50:10, *"For, all the animals of the forest are mine, and I own the cattle on a thousand hills."*

Thanks be to God we are beginning to see Africans go out as missionaries, supported by their own churches.

Only a Phone Number

Fred in the Middle East, 2021

As Covid restrictions eased in the Middle East that summer, a housemate and I travelled to a town of about 130,000 people where there are no known followers of Jesus. Our only contact was a phone number for someone who had ordered a Bible online. I texted his number in the morning and had no response. In the afternoon, as we walked down one of the main streets, a guy randomly invited us to have tea. We sat down and chatted with him. Eventually, I told him that we were looking for a guy and showed him the text and the number. "That's my old number," he said. This was the very man we were hoping to meet! God had put us together. We spent the day with him, sharing the gospel.

The God of the Impossible

Melita Mohr, 2015

We had completed two terms in Indonesia and our home church had welcomed us warmly. But we were carrying a hidden burden—it concerned Tim our youngest child. It also concerned our future as missionaries.

On this beautiful August evening in 1972 Walter and our three older children had gone to enjoy the beauties of Queen Elizabeth Park on Little Mountain, our favourite park with beautiful trees, well-groomed shrubs, manicured beds of colourful flowers, and good walking paths. From the vantage point of the park, the high rises of downtown Vancouver unfold like a rolled-out carpet toward the majestic snow-capped mountain peaks rising high toward heaven.

I had chosen to stay home that evening. I was in our small basement apartment with four-year-old Tim. Tim was tired and I didn't think he was ready for another outing. I had just put him to bed and he quickly fell asleep. My heart was heavy and a feeling of depression settled over me. My thoughts were centred on my dear Tim.

I stood beside his bed and watched him breathing peacefully. I was thinking about the findings. We had made many visits to the Children's Diagnostic Centre. We had been probed with many questions. Tim had been put through an array of rigorous tests. And just a few days ago we had been briefed on the results. They were puzzling. The ECG test showed that his brain was normal. Chromosome counts were normal. He had a healthy body. However, the news was not good. Tim would need to be placed in a special school for retarded children. Perhaps he might learn to speak a few words. But he would never be normal. He would never be independent. There was no known cause and also no known cure.

In my pain I cried out, "God, what hope is there for this child? Father, what future does he have?" Tears were rolling down my cheeks, "Such a beautiful child and he sleeps so peacefully yet what will become of him?" In the stillness an audible voice broke through. I knew it was the Lord. This was a voice of comfort and assurance, "I am the God of the impossible!"

Now there were three of us: Tim sleeping so peacefully; myself—a broken-hearted mother grieving for her child; and the Eternal God whose voice was calming my troubled heart. But what could these words mean? What was I to understand from that soothing voice? Was this a promise of a miracle healing? Was this a promise of special grace? Was this a promise of special strength? I still ponder those words and I still wonder. But hearing his voice and knowing God cared made such a difference.

Walter, Philip, Kathleen and Danny returned and their happy chatter changed the scene. But that voice, those words, they lingered on and are still with me. I still hear them deep within when my heart listens to his. Of course, I shared them with Walter but they were spoken to me. They were for me.

Tim has been prayed for by many people. Many remedies and programs have been proposed and we have tried some of them. Some of God's servants have placed their hands on his head and believed for healing. Tim and I sat within fifteen yards of where Kathryn Kuhlman stood as she ministered to many thousands in the Pacific Colosseum in 1974. I saw miracles, some rose from wheelchairs and walked and some even ran. Tim was not among those that received God's touch. The prognosis given to us at the diagnostic centre when he was four years old still holds true. He has a healthy body but healing of the mind has not come. Is it autism? Is it brain damage? What and why, only God knows.

Timmy is now a grown man who recently celebrated his 47th birthday. Much has changed and much is still the same. At age 29 he moved into a Christian Horizons group home and became part of a new family. He is generally a happy young man. He loves music. He loves long walks but someone needs to be with him or he would not find his way home. He enjoys family, food, fellowship, and birthdays. He lives with four other young men who also have special needs. He comes to our home almost every weekend. Sometimes he jumps for joy when he sees us. More often he acts as though we are not all that special so why get excited. He knows that he is loved.

He enjoys the weekly Friendship Club held at Immanuel Christian Reformed Church. He comes to church with us and stays for a meal or two. He loves going with us for a week of holidays. His needs are supplied. He fits in well both at his Christian Horizons home and at our home. When he has been home with us for a few hours he might say, "Timmy go home." When we do not come to get him from his Christian Horizons home he also says, "Timmy go home." Does he know what it means? We are not sure. Although his words are few, he understands much of what we ask of him.

"The God of the impossible!" The troubled virgin Mary heard rather similar words. To her the angel said, *"Fear not!"* then added, *"For nothing is impossible with God."* And nothing is. His grace was sufficient for Mary and his grace has been sufficient for me. I needed to learn to cast my cares on the Lord and leave them there.

And a new day is coming for both of us. Tim will speak well on that day when God makes everything new. Then he will be in his forever home. And we will fully understand all unanswered questions. I will also understand what God meant when he spoke those words of hope and assurance. He truly is the God of the impossible. He is the God of miracles!

The Ultimate Goal

Anonymous in Asia, 2018

My tutor and I were meeting several times a week during my husband's school break. We figured I could do a language-intensive season of four weeks, meeting four hours per day five days a week while he was off school. It was a brilliant plan. My tutor was asking more questions, becoming curious about my life, warming-up and turning into an enjoyable companion. This was not the case when I first hired her. In our line of work: we are dependent on helpers because we begin without cultural or language understanding. Finding suitable helpers is part of the walk of faith. We always pray for God to provide just the right helper. I had met with a few other gals, offered good pay, and yet they seemed less than enthusiastic about tutoring and cancelled.

An expat friend said he had a student who could be a good choice. Her English was excellent and she hoped to become a foreign language teacher some day. From the first moment I met her she was harsh and critical. She often tried to teach me unhelpful slang or crass words. She showed up though, and was highly punctual. I kept praying for her while wanting to replace her but the Lord gave me the willingness to persevere. Slowly but surely through a variety of conversations and special events she warmed up and heard more about Jesus.

Once she asked me, "Why are you and your husband so joyful and kind to each other? I've never met another couple like you." Jay and I believe the heart of our ministry is our marriage. It thrilled me to explain our marriage to her. We talked about humility, mutual service, submission, repentance, forgiveness and having the Lord as our guide. She was amazed.

At our fourth meeting, a waiter awkwardly asked us to sit at a specific table. There were two cameras set up beside that table. We insisted that we pick our own spot. This was a classic attempt to spy on our meeting. We couldn't meet at our apartment because the police were visiting frequently and our visitors had to be registered. The next week we were going to study some sensitive material and when we sat down to begin, I clearly heard in my mind, "the man beside you speaks English, do not talk about this topic, he is not safe." I promptly changed the topic. Half an hour later he approached our table. He had heard some English and wanted to join the conversation. We can always trust the Lord to guide us.

One week into the school break we got a call from our friends who lived in the same apartment block, "We were just given 48 hours to leave the neighbourhood, to move to another part of the city." An hour later we got a call from the police that we needed to go into the office with our documents at two in the afternoon. With two hours looming ahead of us, we fully expected that we too would be evicted from the neighbourhood. As we walked past tanks and trucks full of soldiers our hearts sank. This was the neighbourhood we loved, and that housed our people. Furthermore, if we moved, we would have to live on campus which was locked-down at that point. This would halt my frequent meetings with my tutor. We prayed and asked the Lord for help, but had resigned ourselves to the impending move. We went to the office. They said, "We were going to tell you to move away but we decided you can stay until the school break is over, then you will need to move onto campus."

My mom messaged me a few hours later, "Are you okay? Your friend texted me that she was wakened in the night to pray for you. She interceded for you for two hours." We were in awe when we relayed the events of that day.

The extra month afforded my tutor and I precious hours of deep and intentional discussion and Biblical study. Then one day, a week after we moved into the campus dormitory, she told me she had become a Christian the night before. She expressed to my husband and I that she suddenly sees the world and her life and others in a whole new light.

This young woman has proven to be a faithful disciple and passionate evangelist. In her first week of being a Christian she shared with her roommates with tears and repentance for having been a callous and unkind roommate, which resulted in one of her roommates finding Christ. She has proved to be a faithful and passionate disciple, and we've stayed in touch.

Be faithful to trust he will bring the right people for his purposes. She's the evangelist who got to stay when I had to leave. Language acquisition wasn't the ultimate goal and never will be.

Yunus Comes to the Lord

Fred in the Middle East, 2018

"I will give you a new heart and put a new spirit in you; I will remove from you your heart of stone and give you a heart of flesh. And I will put my Spirit in you and move you to follow my decrees and be careful to keep my laws." Ezekiel 36: 26-27

In church in Canada, before I left for the Middle East, I tried to sit beside people who I didn't know. My intention was to make new friends and share Christ with them. I never knew, I could be sitting beside a lukewarm Christian or a non-believer.

This practice is something I continued to do in the Middle East. One Sunday, I sat beside a man in the corner. During the sermon about Jonah and the whale, this fellow started crying.

After the service, I was able to chat with him and he said that his name was Yunus which translates to Jonah. The sermon touched him. God used it to soften his heart of stone. That week he had intended to commit suicide, but he heard a voice telling him to go find a church. Our church was the first that came up online. I was able to take him to the front and our pastor led him to the Lord.

I was with him during his baptism and he is still following the Lord today.

One of Christ's Trophies

Walter Mohr in Tajikistan, 2001

Zuchra was an Uzbek orphan whose life was transformed because God sent a dream. Her face glowed. Meeting her was an unforgettable experience. I met her in April 2001 at an evening house fellowship in Dushanbe, Tajikistan. Zuchra had come with her two lovely children. Her daughter was 13 and her son was 8. I was deeply moved as she gave her testimony. Here is her amazing story of God's grace.

Zuchra never knew her father. As an orphan her only hope for survival was the life of the streets. She learned the art of sorcery—it helped to put food on the table. She also became an alcoholic and an adulteress. Although she identified as a Muslim, she never prayed, fasted or visited a mosque. Increasingly the darkness of her lifestyle overwhelmed her. All she felt and knew was guilt, despair and hopelessness. Why do I do this? Why keep on living? Why not end it all?

One day she made a firm decision. I will end it all. As she was contemplating this act of desperation another painful fact confronted her. What will happen to my children? She decided that since she brought these children into the world; to save them from lives of shame and misery, she must first kill her children. So very deliberately she planned their murder and her own suicide.

But then God sent a vivid dream. She saw Jesus sitting on a throne. Instinctively she knew it was Jesus. How she knew that she could not tell. Jesus had a crown on his head and wore royal robes. She was in the throne room and it was awesome. The next scene was frightening. Jesus was holding a double-edged sword pointing upward in his right hand. As her eyes followed the shaft upward it became a cross. She woke with a start. She knew there was no cross in Islam – it is hated symbol. What did the dream mean?

In the morning, she hastened to tell her Russian Orthodox neighbour her dream. Her response was simply, "I do not know what it means Zuchra, but this I know, your life will change." She kept telling and retelling her dream but no one could give her a satisfying interpretation. Of course she did not pursue her evil plans.

One day she met a Korean pastor and told him her dream. He said I can interpret that dream. God sent you a beautiful message. Zuchra, it is a very clear message. The Jesus you recognized is the Messiah mentioned often in the Koran. And he is a king, in fact he is the King above all kings. And as you saw, he is seated on a throne in heaven. He reigns with justice and the sword in his hand means that he judges sin and all evil deeds.

But the good news is this. He judges with mercy and love. He loves you Zuchra and he died for you on that cross. He actually took the punishment you deserve. He loves you so much that he sent you this dream. He knew what you were planning and he stepped in to save you. Yes, Jesus already saved your life and the lives of your children. But he also wants to save your soul and forgive your sins. That is why he died on the cross. Never forget he loves you and he loves your children. He loves you very much. You are very special to Jesus.

"With a grateful heart I immediately asked Jesus to forgive me for my many sins. And He did." Zuchra continued, "He also gave me a new heart and another chance at life." The glow on Zuchra's face confirmed the change she had experienced. Now Zuchra does not live on the streets. She serves Jesus and shares of his love to all who will listen. And praise God both of her children also follow Jesus.

When she ended her story both Zuchra and I had tears in our eyes. I gave her a hug and she said, "Walter, will you be my father?" Quickly I replied, "Zuchra, you already have a Father. You certainly can think of me as your father this evening but I cannot stay in Dushanbe. Remember you have a Heavenly Father who loves you, cares for you and will never leave you. He will stay with you."

Paul said it so well, *"If anyone is in Christ, he is a new creation."* Zuchra is one of Christ's trophies.

XI

Meeting Practical Needs

What good is it, my brothers, if someone says he has faith but does not have works? Can that faith save him? If a brother or sister is poorly clothed and lacking in daily food, and one of you says to them, "Go in peace, be warmed and filled," without giving them the things needed for the body, what good is that? So also, faith by itself, if it does not have works, is dead.
James 2:14-17

"Go in peace, be warmed and filled" are just empty words to people living miserable unproductive lives without work; or to drug addicts who need rehabilitation; to foreign students who need community; to people who need relief from toothaches; or people with mysterious illnesses in need of healing. WEC Missionaries can't be all things to all people, but sometimes God presents them with the opportunity to share about him while they are addressing basic needs.

A God Idea

Ruth in East Asia, 2000's

Many people, especially women, were living miserable unproductive lives in my country of service. I wanted a way to restore independence and dignity to their lives. The head person at a women's organization agreed to help. God gave us the idea to introduce microloans.

We began small with six microloans. Authorities were sceptical, so I used personal funds. The goal was to give poor families ownership over their lives. All six families in the pilot project repaid their loans. Officials had to admit the success was phenomenal. Each of the pilot families went into the second year of the loan program with a refined plan and we immediately expanded to help 30 new families, with some individual projects and some larger community loan programs.

This is how the program worked. The loans were made for one year. During this time all children in the family were sponsored in school. The businesses we helped to create were varied. At the end of the year the money was repaid and we examined each business and extended it in ways to make it more independent. Then the money was re-loaned for a second year and the entrepreneurs supported their own children in school. The third year, when money was repaid, it was given to another family. Because of this, the microloans continue to roll over. My partner in the women's association helped with choosing the families. She and her staff and I worked as a team.

Once the loan program was firmly established, 50 loans were given out at different times of the year, so not all loans matured at the same time. This made my work easier and gave me more time to connect. There were different projects: a cloth-making loom business; fish-pond farms; pig raising; cheese, milk and yogurt businesses; spiceries; apple farms; a greenhouse vegetable business; chickens and egg businesses; a sewing business to name a few.

Loan repayment time provided opportunity to speak into the lives of each of these families. Smiling women came, hands stretched out with money to repay the small loans that had changed their lives. Hopefully the little about God I could share at that time created readiness to receive Jesus into their hearts.

During the times of my visiting and helping them to find the best ways to be successful, we built loving, caring relationships. I didn't share the gospel while money was still owed. I didn't want to encourage rice Christians. When the money was paid back, the relationship was then rich for sharing. If anyone showed an eagerness to hear more, I connected them with local underground Christians who could take the next step.

Bringing Christ to the Drug Pits of Madrid

José Garcia in Spain, 2020's

I met Barbara several years ago in the drug area where thousands of addicts gather. She was in bad shape, but still managed to have a place to live together with her boyfriend. Things got ugly and she admitted that her boyfriend would constantly beat her. We suggested she leave him and join our rehabilitation program, but she declined.

One day in an unexpected twist, a car driven by another addict ran her over. This put her in the hospital for several months which kept her safe from her boyfriend. After her recovery, instead of returning to the abusive relationship or coming to be rehabilitated, she fled to the coastal city of Valencia, where she continued to do drugs. She had escaped from her boyfriend, but still had the chains of drugs in her life. This addiction eventually left her broke and devastated.

At this point, Barbara wanted to come back to Madrid to join our rehabilitation program. She had no money, but felt something inside telling her to go to the bus station. Other voices were telling her to end her life. She sat down at a table at the station and wept. When she opened her eyes some minutes later, she saw an envelope with enough money inside for a ticket to Madrid.

She returned to Madrid, joined our program at Betel and God radically changed her life in these last two years. She is now married to a loving man she met in the program and with whom she serves the Lord. She now goes back to the drug areas and preaches about the change that only God can make.

Food, Fun and Faith

Leah de Vos in Canada, 2021

In 2021, I launched a hospitality ministry to international students in Hamilton. Each week I invited a new female student to my place. I would share my testimony and the from-creation-to-Christ story. The interactions with the students were very positive, especially since most of them had little familiarity with the concept of God. I also passed along some reading material to those who wanted to learn more.

I hosted larger events as well. We did a Chinese hotpot party and a dumpling party. The Chinese students made the dumpling batter by hand and showed the rest of us how to put the filling inside and fold them properly—what a fun experience! After that meal, I shared a story that highlights blessing which is a significant theme in Chinese culture. My story was about God fulfilling his promise of blessing his people by sending Jesus. Later in the evening, when I asked for responses to the message, one of the students poured out his heart, sharing his uncertainty about the existence of God in an evil and broken world. He wanted to believe there is a God who cares.

I have since moved from Hamilton to St. Catharines, and am working with students in the universities in this area, planning events such as hikes, a sugar bush tour, and a potluck supper. Having fun together helps people become more comfortable with one another.

Serving as a Dentist

Helen Krueger in Côte d'Ivoire, 1944-1996

Once the people found out that the white lady was able to pull teeth the word passed from village to village. There were no dentists in our area and most people didn't have strong string or a set of pliers to pull a tooth. When our car arrived in a village, a line-up would form. We would ask the dental patients to wait until after our meeting. I said if they would listen to the message about God, I would pull their teeth.

Often, the people would come one by one all afternoon. Each time I would have to get the forceps and with no anaesthetic, pull teeth. They would rinse their mouths with a salty mouthwash afterwards.

One man had an infected back molar which had kept him from sleeping and eating for several days. I had a look and told him that it would be very difficult, as this tooth did not seem the least bit loose. He begged me to try, so a little stool was brought for him to sit on and I pushed the forceps down, just as the dentist in Toronto had taught us. I pulled with all my strength until I actually felt dizzy. I pushed his head down with my left hand to keep him from rising up and pulled with my right. I was quite strong but had no success. At one point I stopped, but although the process was very painful for him, he asked me to keep trying. Well, I got my breath back and breathed a prayer and tried again and finally the tooth came out. What a happy man he was and with a mouth full of blood he tried to hug me. Then came the blessings that Muslims like to bestow: may you have a long life; may Allah cause you to remain a long time in our country; may you prosper; and may you have many children.

For forty years in that area, I was the only person to pull teeth. The government finally brought in a real dentist with a diploma. He had a real office with a modern dental chair, which was a gift from Israel. At this point I was told not to pull any more teeth because I did not have a diploma. It was upsetting because many people still came to have a tooth pulled and I had to refuse them and direct them to the dentist who charged ten dollars. The charge was to cover the cost of the shot and disinfectant. Many could not afford the ten dollars.

Finally, out of compassion, the government told me that I could pull teeth for those who did not have the money to pay the dentist.

Chosen to Go *by Helen Krueger, pages 68-9.*

The Zawadi challenge

Nancy Wood in the Democratic Republic of the Congo, 1973

When Philip and I started work in Nyankunde in the Democratic Republic of the Congo in September 1973, I was given responsibility for 24 beds in the pediatric ward and 24 in the adult female ward. Most of the time all the beds were full.

One afternoon on my rounds I discovered a new patient in bed 24, just at the entry on my right, a girl, about ten years old, Zawadi by name. She had been brought in by a Swiss nurse who often checked on people who were living in the ramshackle motel beside the hospital.

If Zawadi had lived in Old Testament times, she would have been given a diagnosis of leprosy as was Miriam in Numbers 12:10 for *"her skin was white as snow."* We knew this wasn't leprosy which usually presents with one reddish blotch on the skin of a black person. But what was it? In any case dear Zawadi was being pursued by a swarm of flies attracted by her weeping grey-white skin. The Swiss nurse, Marie Jeanne realized that Zawadi needed to be protected by a mosquito net which the hospital could provide. Very soon Zawadi was comfortably installed in bed with clean sheets under the mosquito net.

I was left with the dilemma of being her doctor and needing to prescribe something for her total body disease, including her tender scalp under her thick black curls. I decided on an anti-fungal medicine once a day, and an antibiotic once a day, and then some ointments for the nursing students to apply to her skin after her daily bucket bath. They were encouraged to include her head and hair in her daily bath. One week, two weeks, three weeks....

In a month Zawadi's skin was virtually healed but no progress had been made on her tender head. I was sure she did not want to stay in hospital any longer and the nursing students had done their best. What was I prepared to do? I decided to discharge Zawadi from the hospital on the condition that she would walk up the gravel hill to my house every afternoon at four so that I could continue to give her anti-fungal and antibacterial pills, and especially to wash her hair. Fortunately, we had an outside laundry basin with running water, a luxury in itself. I had several soaps and shampoos to try on her hair but without success. Her hair was growing quite well and so about once a month I trimmed it for her but still the tangled matted hair remained. Actually, her tender scalp was thoroughly involved.

Finally, after about six months of daily treatments, the Lord gave me a bright idea. After a shampoo and a trim, I sent her down to the hospital with a note to one of the student nurses on duty, to cover her scalp with Methylene Blue which we often used on scrapes and cuts that no longer needed a bandage. With continued pills for bacteria and fungus, a week of treatments was encouraging. Another trim of her black curls, more Methylene Blue every day and further improvement in the second week. Finally, after four weeks of daily shampoos, daily pills, frequent trims and a daily application of Methylene Blue, we could call her scalp healthy.

Several years later, I saw Zawadi one afternoon walking in front of the hospital clearly on her way to the Tuesday Bible study at the local church. She was cleanly dressed, her skin was healthy, her curls were thick and healthy and she had her Bible tucked under her arm.

Praise God for doing the impossible.

XII

God Provides

See how the flowers of the field grow. They do not labour or spin. Yet I tell you that not even Solomon in all his splendor was dressed like one of these. If that is how God clothes the grass of the field, which is here today and tomorrow is thrown into the fire, will he not much more clothe you—you of little faith? So do not worry, saying, 'What shall we eat?' or 'What shall we drink?' or 'What shall we wear?' For the pagans run after all these things, and your heavenly Father knows that you need them. But seek first his kingdom and his righteousness, and all these things will be given to you as well.

Matthew 6:28b–33

One of the four pillars of WEC is faith. If you live by faith, you know that what God says in his Word is true. WEC workers know that if they seek first his kingdom and his righteousness, he'll take care of them just like he cares for the birds and the flowers. Whether it's enough support to go to the field, a place to live, airline tickets, or tuition fees, God provides one way or another.

A Home on the Mountain

Patty Hines at WEC Canada headquarters, 2013

Our biggest need, looking toward retirement, was to have a home of our own, where our children and grandchildren would be able to visit comfortably. In January of 2013 we got a call from one of our donors who wanted to help us purchase a place. He was moving out of his own large house to a smaller condo, and said that he would love to lend us a down-payment on a home in Hamilton. If and when he needed a nursing home, he would want the money back. We were flabbergasted at his offer. With that generous down-payment and our savings, we began the hunt for a house.

By June of that year, we had found nothing that suited our layout needs, and our pocketbook. Our directors took a car ride with us during conference that year to view some of the places we had seen. At that time, they encouraged us to look up on Hamilton Mountain away from the smoke stacks, where the price was less affordable, but the location was more amenable to Jon's allergies. I was a bit anxious about the prices up on the mountain, but we continued to look. By then, one of our fellow workers also volunteered financial help with the project.

In August of 2013 we found a promising listing on the computer. Would it still be available for us after the weekend? I felt confident that it would and it was. The house had the perfect layout for seniors and was close to WEC headquarters where we worked. We met with the realtor that week to sign the papers to purchase our small home on 'the mountain'.

God has been faithful to us since 2013 when we purchased the home. We have made a few improvements to it, and we will continue to do so yearly, as God provides. This home is just what we needed at the right time. He is so faithful.

God is Able

Juan Arvelo in Spain, 2019

To complete my Theory and Practice of Ethnodoxology course from the Master's program in World Arts I had to get to Dallas, Texas for a week-long intensive component on-campus. I didn't have the funds to go. As the days went by, I was still lacking the money to book the air ticket. One evening my wife and I were ready to use our credit card to pay for it but, literally, God stopped us. The day before the trip I still didn't have the money, but we had the certainty that God was about to surprise us. And he did.

That afternoon, I decided to pack my suitcases trusting that God would open a door for me. When I finished packing, I sat down on the sofa waiting for God to intervene. Minutes later I received an email from the professor asking for my arrival details. I explained that I was still waiting on God for his provision to book the ticket, and she replied, "We have just received an offering for a special fund for cases such as these so, tell me how much you need. We are paying your ticket."

I couldn't believe my ears. My wife was in tears when she heard the news. God is so good. The following day was surreal; just hours before, I didn't have the money to go to Dallas but then, I was seated on an airplane on my way to Dallas. God is able!"

Never Had a Big Bank Account

Clarence and Lucille Knapp in Burkina Faso, 1950's

We can testify to God's gracious supply of all our needs in many miraculous ways throughout our almost 62 years together. We never had a big bank account but we could always count on God. One year when our two oldest children were with us, we were preparing to go home for a furlough and needed to purchase plane tickets. I had booked the tickets well in advance but two weeks before our flying date we still did not have sufficient funds to pay for the tickets. Finally on our last mail day before we needed to leave for Bobo Diolasso (five hours away) to catch the plane, I again went to the post office. I was about to leave when the manager called me back saying, "You have another letter here that you must sign for." When I arrived home and opened the letter, we found a $1000 cheque inside—exactly the amount we needed to pay for the rest of the trip. You can be sure we all praised and thanked God for his timely gracious provision.

Can I trust God to Provide without my Help?

Caroline Brown, 1997

We were preparing to join WEC and go overseas. We had signed up with a realtor to sell our dream house as we readied to move to Hamilton for training before going overseas. But did I have the faith to trust God to provide for our needs, even just the practical financial needs let alone all the other needs?

WEC has a curious financial policy: its members trust God to provide for their financial needs without their solicitation. I quite liked the faith and finance policy as I disliked the idea of asking others for money, and if God provided then it showed his leading in this endeavour. But could I live by it? How does it work in practice? How will people know to give if I don't ask? Can I trust God in this?

It was mid-March, my husband, Mick was in New Orleans for the week with work. I was home on our acreage, about 20 kilometres outside of Calgary. Our house was listed on Tuesday and people wanted to come and view it by the weekend. But on Wednesday morning, a sudden snowfall left the driveway, all 125 metres of it, covered in 30 to 90 centimetres of snow, and no hope of a thaw. The realtor told me to get it cleared, no car could get in or out. I wondered how. Perhaps I could hire a contractor, but then I sensed God telling me to trust him on this. He could clear the drive without my asking anyone else, if I would pray about it, and with the children too. I was none to happy about the idea of including the children in the prayer, but my limited faith was sufficient to make me go through with it. We prayed and waited.

The next day there was still a beautiful view of the undisturbed snow that made it difficult to even discern where the drive was. If it wasn't cleared today then I would have to resort to calling in a contractor, but could I trust God to provide without my asking? That afternoon as I sat down to read my Bible and pray, I heard a noise; a large tractor equipped with a snowplow was heading towards the house leaving a cleared path. I ran out to thank the driver, told him he was an answer to prayer and asked who he was. He replied, "Greg, I was just passing." I didn't know him. He worked at a nearby ranch and just happened to be passing and saw a need. This had never happened before in the seven years that we had lived there.

It was a huge lesson and encouragement to me. I could trust God to provide for the needs of my family, even without my soliciting for funds. My five-year-old son's response to this miracle showed much greater faith than I had, "God always answers prayer. Now I can go to Awana (Bible club for children) today!"

The house sold that very weekend.

Unplanned Journey and Unimagined Blessings

Mick Brown in Türkiye, 2001

I didn't plan or organize anything. My colleague who was setting up a faith tourism company was the sort to say 'yes' to everything. You might call it faith but there was a distinct component of optimistic disorganization. In 2001, he'd said yes to facilitating a tour of early Christian sites in Türkiye for a group of Americans. He was well enough organized to ask me to be the driver and translator for the group while he was off doing something else.

Thankfully the leader of the American 'group' had put together the itinerary and with help from my colleague they had already worked out what they were doing and where they were going to be staying. My work started with driving a rented minibus 1,000 kilometres from my base to a hotel in Kars in North East Türkiye where I met them.

It was an interesting group and an interesting meeting. The group had shrunk since its original inception and the remnant was the main organizer, his wife and daughter and a friend of the family. The friend would have come with her husband but he died some weeks before the trip. She decided, with encouragement from her friends, that she should come anyway.

The group leader turned out to be a keen Christian born the same year as myself and both of us were quite fit, but apart from that we were 'chalk and cheese' as the British in me would say. He was a large, loud, forthright extrovert American—I'm the antithesis. I was exposed to our differences early on. He would always sit in the front passenger seat with the only other male in the group, me. From there he would occasionally have loud heated arguments with his wife concerning trip options. Graciously he explained to me that this was their normal means of coming to an agreement; this appeared to be true and did not result in the same conflict that I know would have resulted in my marriage had the same discussion happened. Strangely enough it quickly became apparent that we were going to get on well and to enjoy each other's company; he liked the fact that we could laugh at and make fun of each other. My excitement at seeing a Hoopoe and racing around to get a good shot of it were a particular source of amusement: he also likes to shoot birds but uses a gun rather than a camera. Trips to famous places such as Ani, Mount Ararat, Mor Gabriel, and Cappadocia (to name just a few) with many hours of driving and talking in between resulted in a bond that remains to this day, about twenty years on.

This first trip took place in our late forties and so he decided that we should go to the summit of Mount Ararat (5,137 metres in elevation) while we were still young enough, this happened about four years later. A third trip, a few years later, involved visiting sites in Armenia and then hiking a series of peaks (about 4,000 metres in elevation) around an extinct volcano; this trip included my wife who elected to hike with us as opposed to shopping in Istanbul which is what the other ladies did.

This association resulted in my experiencing more of the wonders in the land of Türkiye, but more significant was the relationship that I and then my family were able to build with this American family. Their interest in missions included support of the principal of a school in Türkiye where we had decided to send our children. When the family heard our children were going to start at the school they helped us with the not insignificant tuition costs, and they have continued to financially support us. Later when our daughter had graduated from high school and needed an internship working with animals for her university studies, they helped by arranging a placement at a veterinary clinic close to them, hosted her at their house and even loaned her their daughter's car. Perhaps the greatest evidence of this man's friendship to me is that he prays daily for us and our unbelieving relatives.

My unplanned excursion resulted in blessings *"far beyond what I might have asked or imagined"* as per Paul's prayer in Ephesians 3:20. I have experienced God's generous provision in other ways, but this was probably the most enjoyable and unexpected.

God's Wonderful Supply

Edith Seager (Shingler) to India, 1945

Beth Allinger and I had been called to India. I had approximately $180 in my account. One day a friend, a hard-working farmer, came in and gave me a check for $420, which brought it up to $600.

I had been going to my dentist for about a year and had a lot of work done which amounted to $75. The dentist, a Christian, had prayed about it and after a while he said, "I believe I have the mind of the Lord. Whatever gift of money given to you for your going to the field, whether it be 50 cents or 50 dollars, it will cover my fee. I realize that if it is only 50 cents it will be a loss, but not a loss as God is no man's debtor."

I walked out of his office to fulfill a luncheon engagement. There a lady put her hand into her purse and said she wanted to give me my street car tickets, and she handed me two dollars. I told the dentist about this and he said, "That is what we told the Lord and that is what it shall be, just send me the two dollars and we'll call the bill paid."

Then, the last day before leaving, a widow came in to see me and gave me $300 and a check of $200 from her son whom I did not know. Her son also brought a gift of $50 for Beth Allinger. That afternoon Beth and I were asked to see a person who wished to give us a gift. They explained that they had some money set aside for an obligation but felt that God would have them give it to us and trust him when the need arose. It was a check for $1,200. This amount was what we needed to go on our journey.

Beth Allinger to India, 1945

The morning of February 28th my account was barely $300 for my passage to India. That afternoon word came that Edith and I were to proceed to Philadelphia at once because our sailing had been advanced from March 16th to March 5th. Part of that $300 came in through a friend who had recently given herself to the Lord for all he had for her. She was a nurse and felt led to give me her whole check, $111.08, for India. At a meeting in a Baptist church that night I received $42 toward my passage. Upon arriving home, an elderly widow who had a little bake-shop, and her daughter brought $225 for the outgoing party. At our last meeting in the Toronto headquarters, it was announced at the breakfast table that $150 had been put into my account anonymously. Then Edith's country friends, whom I had never met before, gave me $50. Two hours before we were to leave, we received a most unexpected gift of $1,200 to be divided between us, making it possible for us to go away with praise to God for the miracles that he had wrought.

XIII

God Hears and Answers Our Prayers

"If you believe, you will receive whatever you ask for in prayer."
Matthew 21:22

Whether the prayers are spoken by the missionary, the supporter of the missionary, a new believer or an unbeliever, God answers prayers and he does it in very creative and interesting ways. In the following stories, he sends a random bottle of fresh water to a thirsty missionary; he sends a missionary to answer the prayer of an unbeliever; he sends a set of angels to missionaries stuck in the desert; he sends a little boy to reassure his missionary teacher; and he uses the answer of one prayer as the answer to another. He uses an accident, resurrection buns, and soldiers. No prayer is too small or too big—God has the ability and the desire to answer each prayer.

A Bottle with a Message

Esther in the Middle East, 2006

On my day off work, I decided to go to the beach with a friend for refreshment and time with God. We drove 45 minutes to the beach. Then to get to a private area, we walked another 45 minutes along rugged terrain and sand dunes in 35-degree temperature and high humidity.

When we finally reached our destination, I realised I hadn't brought enough water to last the day. I didn't tell my friend because I felt silly neglecting something so basic. In this hot, humid country, it was essential to keep hydrated.

I decided to pray about my dilemma. I spent some time walking along the beach wading in the waters, enjoying the waves and stillness. As I prayed, I saw something bobbing up and down, jostled by the waves. As it came closer, I recognized the thing as a bottle. Maybe there was a message inside.

The bottle came right to me. There was seaweed around its neck and it appeared to be full of water. I wasn't sure if this was sea water or fresh water, but when I opened the cap and took a sip, I tasted sweet fresh water! God had heard my prayer and this was his amazing answer.

Darkness is as Light to God

Beth in Asia, 2023

We found a park where women who speak our new language meet during the limited hours in the day when women are free for visiting. In the hot months, the only time is after sunset. Sunset certainly cools the temperature, but it also makes it almost impossible to spot women wearing black.

Late one evening we somewhat reluctantly went out to fulfill our routine of several rotations around the track in this park. On one of these laps, a young lady came out of the dark and told us, "My mom knows you." We followed her to where her mom (we weren't sure who that was) was sitting under a tree.

We joined the mom on the ground. We had met her before—a refugee from a neighbouring country. She was quite pregnant. With the pleasantries out of the way, and her children distracted by play, she opened up her black covering so we could see her clothes underneath which had a huge rip right over the belly. She told us of the abuse she was experiencing from some of the men in her home. We tried to listen and understand, though with our limited knowledge of the language, we didn't comprehend all the complexities. One of us told her, in our simple way, unsure of exactly how to love her and show our care, "God sees everything." That led her to tell us how that evening, instead of covering herself up for prayers, she exposed her torn clothes and asked God, "Do you see this?"

We were so thankful that we had left our home that evening to deliver the answer to her prayer. Realizing that God heard her cry, opened her up to listening to more of the things we longed to share with her. The next time we saw her in that park, she told the other ladies we were followers of Jesus. Subsequently, she had her child and returned to the shadows of her original country. We believe that like Mary, she is *"treasuring all these things up in her heart."*

Angels to the Rescue

Philip Wood in the Sahara, 1977

The Leprosy Mission in England gifted our Nebobongo Hospital in the Congo with a new Land Rover. David Burnett and I were recruited to drive this vehicle across the Sahara to its destination. We did the journey in three weeks, thanks to the prayers of our supporters and a big box on our roof rack that looked like a coffin. At almost every frontier a customs officer would come over to ask, "What do you have in that box?"

"Oh, come and see," I would say.

We would climb up the ladder at the back of our new vehicle and pry open the lid. Inside was a large operating room light. "Oh, okay off you go," the customs officer would say, not one bit curious about our new vehicle.

Our one major difficulty was a huge sand dune in northern Niger. On foot, we climbed up to the top ridge to see if we could possibly drive round the end of it, but the dune stretched for as far as we could see in both directions. We had to go over it. Our heavily laden vehicle sank into the dry sand in no time at all. We had to dig ourselves out and place sand ladders to get ourselves some ten metres further where we would have to start digging again. We were soon exhausted in this process and sat down in the shade of the Land Rover to rest.

Then I remembered we had not prayed. Together we asked for the Lord's help and not five minutes later a bright red Land Cruiser drove up. A young couple were inside but we were astonished to see that they seemed to be in an empty vehicle. What, no Jerry cans of water or fuel, no camping equipment?

Being unladen they could easily drive up and over the sand. They had a winch as we did and by hooking the two winches together, they could winch us over the dune. They then immediately took off and we had no opportunity to get to know them. I am sure they were angels. Thank you, Lord.

Little Bright Eyes

Linda Nagel in Côte d'Ivoire, 1972

I asked the Lord to help me make the lesson simple and culturally relevant so the younger children in my noon class would understand. Later that afternoon, in another school in the same town, I was in the middle of giving an identical lesson when a bright-eyed little boy stepped in. I recognized him as one of the children who had attended the earlier class. He listened intently as though he was hearing the story for the first time.

The flannelgraph lesson depicted two boys approaching the gates of heaven. One boy said he was sure he could enter because he had been so good, but the door didn't open. The second boy said he was a sinner but had asked Jesus to forgive him. The door opened. I asked the question, "Why didn't the door open for the first boy?"

Little bright eyes from the noon class waved his hand in the air eager to answer. I wanted the others to respond first, but they hesitated so the little fellow piped up, "Because he did not open his heart to Jesus and ask him to forgive him of his sins." The other children, who were older, looked in amazement at the little boy. I didn't give away the secret that this was the second time he heard the lesson, and then the Lord reminded me, "This is the answer to your morning prayer." If this little boy got the message probably the others did too.

***Just to be Clay** (2021) by Linda Nagel, page 107.*

Matters of Life and Death

Ruth in East Asia, 2000's

Often, we travelled to take clothes and food into the high mountains where children were dying for lack of basic needs. On one such expedition, we had to take horses because the path was so narrow and the loose pebbles made it dangerous to walk. On the way up a mountainside, as we navigated an extremely narrow part of the path, my horse's front hoof dropped into a sink hole under the pebble bed. The horse reared up, and threw me off over the edge of the path. The nationals were in a panic, fearful of losing their first foreigner to the bottom of the deep gorge.

I was able to hang on by my fingers until they pulled me up. I don't remember thinking, "I wish I had more money." I only remember the words, "Thank you God that there are so many people praying for me."

Our Son's Birth

Melissa Swan in Chad 2022

While in Abéché, Chad, Central Africa, Jeremy and I were excited to discover that we were expecting our sixth child. We prayed with our team and discussed whether we should stay or leave the country to have the baby. We had always dreamed of having a baby overseas. Our other five children had all been born before we went to Chad or on home leave. So, it would be exciting to have the baby born in our home in Abéché—part of living life together with our Chadian friends.

In Abéché we can look around the city when the dust isn't too heavy and from certain places, we can see the mountains that surround the city—not high mountains but rocky mountains. This became special to me in relation to the birth of our baby. We also have a wall all around our house—everyone does. There is an indoor part of the house and an outdoor part of the house and there is a wall that goes around the outdoor part. When we were praying about whether to have our baby at home, with the possible risks involved in not having easy access to good health care, the verse came to me again and again: *"As the mountains surround Jerusalem, so the Lord surrounds his people"* Psalm 125:2. So as the mountains surround Abéché, as the walls surround our house, so the Lord surrounds us and the Lord will care for us and our baby. It was a confirmation of what he wanted and what we wanted too and we were very happy he was giving us the gift of having our baby in our home in Abéché. All the plans and the praying with our team was a special time.

The midwife who happened to be on our team was very helpful in preparing. It was getting close. I was 40 weeks pregnant. With a new baby coming and all those cloth diapers to be washed, it seemed like a good idea to buy a washing machine. Up to then we had always had our clothes washed by hand. Jeremy had seen a small electric washing machine in a shop in town. We could purchase it with a gift a friend had sent. So, one morning before the baby was born, Jeremy and his Chadian friend took the rickshaw to town with the intention of buying the washing machine. On the way they noticed that the city was shutting down. This was very strange—usually the shops are opening in the morning. There was tension in the streets and a lot of young men were walking around. Jeremy's Chadian friend decided they should go home. There was too much unrest. Something was happening. Not long after they got home without the washing machine, there was shooting in the streets. We could hear automatic rifle fire in all directions outside our walls.

A Chadian friend in our house at the time was afraid to go home because she didn't see any of her tribe on the streets and she realized that it was a conflict between her tribe and another tribe. There are many different tribes in our city and they know who they are. When something arises, they sometimes fight each other. My friend kept peeking out the door. She only saw the other tribe walking by. Finally, when it appeared safe, she ventured home.

For two or three days there was unrest, shots, rifle fire, and the streets were closed. We kept remembering, *"As the mountains surround Jerusalem, so the Lord surrounds his people."* Even now when our baby could be born and our midwife couldn't get to us, he was still surrounding us, he was still protecting us, he was still with us. When the shooting finally died down, the cell service was cut. No more communication. The rest of our team didn't know if our baby was being born or not. We knew he wasn't coming but it was stressful for them not knowing and not being allowed to go out in the streets to come see. We made a plan to send a note by a neighbour boy to a friend who knew a back way to the midwife when the time came. It was risky. Thankfully we didn't need to implement our plan. There was no sign of labour and after two or three days the cell service came back on. Our teammates came as soon as the streets were open to see if we were okay. We were fine.

We had a few more days to wait. Jeremy went to town and successfully bought the washing machine. Ten days late, baby Jared arrived. He came quickly while the midwife was still in the rickshaw on the way to our house. All was fine.

Then, ten days after Jared was born, we held a party for the neighbours. This was the cultural thing to do. Friends and neighbours came and we cooked and ate together to celebrate the new baby. Our celebration opened a lot of relationships.

We discovered new meaning to the verse: *"As the mountains surround Jerusalem, so the Lord surrounds his people."*

Rescue from a Burning Car

Jason in Hamilton, 2021

One day toward the end of candidate orientation, my husband Jason and I prayed that the Lord would give us connections with our focus people in Hamilton before we head to the Middle East. The very next day we were driving back from the neighbouring city of Brantford and noticed a burning car in the median. Jason quickly pulled over to see how he could help.

Someone was trapped in the car. The fellow was unconscious on the passenger side—the side hit in the collision. Jason looked into the car from multiple angles trying to figure out how to get the man out. He decided to crawl in from the driver's side and asked one of the other men who had been in the car to hold onto him and pull as soon as Jason had a grip on the unconscious man. I had visions of the burning car exploding before the rescue could be completed, but they got the fellow out and laid him down at a safe distance.

As we waited for emergency crews to arrive, the other men, who had been in the car, gathered around their less-than-conscious friend talking amongst themselves. Imagine our shock to hear the exact dialect of the Middle Eastern language we had been studying. One of the men gave Jason contact information so that we could find out how their friend was doing. We hoped to visit these men when Covid restrictions lifted. We could see a clear connection between this rescued man's situation and the gospel—we are all completely helpless in our sin and need someone from the outside to come in and save us.

When we exchanged phone numbers on that eventful day, we had hoped this would give us an open door into the lives of these men. Six months went by without a word. We thought that despite God so clearly connecting us, we would never see them again. Then one day Jason was out walking with a friend and someone rolled down the window of a car that had pulled up to the stoplight nearby and a young man shouted out, "Hey, you're the guy from the accident." He got out of the car to collect Jason's phone number before taking off again. Amazing that in a city of over 500,000 people that this fellow met and recognized Jason on the street even though the accident had taken place at night.

One evening not long after, Jason connected with a group of young Arab men in a popular park. After hanging out with them for a while, our friend from the accident strolled up and warmly greeted Jason. The members of the group asked him, "How do you know Jason?"

"This is the guy who pulled Samir out of the car," he said. We pray that Jason will have meaningful connections with these young men.

Resurrection Buns

Anonymous in Asia, 2017

My husband packed up his textbooks and we prayed as we often did before he left for school. We would ask the Lord for opportunities to share his love and truth and to bring people who are seeking truth and love to us. As he left in the rain I thought, "I'll make dough for cinnamon buns as a surprise for him." I started the dough and set it out to rise. I was staying in the dormitory with our baby and had tutors set to visit that day.

When my husband got home later in the day, he arrived soaked, but overjoyed. "You will not believe what happened to me today! Is it possible for you to make a big batch of Resurrection Buns tonight or is it too late?"

"Well, yes. I can because I happened to make dough this morning and it's in the fridge." It seemed God in his foreknowledge had put this idea in my mind.

My husband had been praying about how to reach his classmates who were mostly Central Asian foreign students. Since we were in a dormitory, we did have some opportunities to be amongst them and to share, but we needed more opportunities with the others who Jay only saw in class. Well, on this day, the day it rained, the teacher said, "This weekend is three holidays: April Fools' Day, Easter, and a local holiday." She then randomly assigned three students to present the next day about these holidays. Pointing to my husband she said, "You will share about Easter because you're western, and it's not just religion it's also culture." This is why he was so excited; he was given carte blanche to share the Easter story with his classmates. In his creativity, he imagined that we could make resurrection buns as a prop but knew that they are time consuming.

As soon as he relayed this exciting opportunity to me, we rejoiced and thanked God for what was about to be shared. This is the kind of country and classroom where these stories are rarely shared, much less mandated. Then we put on our boots, grabbed our umbrellas and set out to the baking shop to get the ingredients for icing and sprinkles. Being the shrewd little workers that we were, we came up with an intricate design which represented each important element of the Easter story so that we had a cultural excuse to share. We stayed up late into the night putting sprinkles on with tweezers, making each one a perfect design.

The next day Jay went to class expecting he would do his 15-minute presentation. However, the other two students hadn't prepared anything at all! The irritated teacher said, "Then I will give Jay the full class hour to tell us about Easter." Jay passed out the beautiful buns, with little gold-sprinkle studded crosses with crowns on top, and proceeded to share the entire gospel message, including the concept about his kingdom yet to come and how every person in this room (many who were Muslims) would someday stand before the throne and realize that Jesus is Lord. He explained that the buns were cultural tradition, common place food for Easter. He didn't mention that the extra design elements were our new invention, but instead, drawing each design element on the board, told the next part of the story. To his surprise, his language teacher helped with writing out key terms. She had the students write down the terms, take down sentences in the language as "language practice" and copy them into their books. The students ate the sweet buns with hollow centres as they heard the sweetest news; that Jesus Christ is God incarnate, and has paid the price for their sins. The cooperation and support of the teacher was bizarre but a welcomed partnership. Through this, all 26 of Jay's classmates from some of the hardest-to-reach *"Stan"* countries heard the news. The immediate outcome was that we had some of the students come to our room to hear more, and pour out their hearts to us. Jesus tells us to be shrewd as snakes and innocent as doves. We think he was pleased with our cunning and innocent way of sharing about him. Who knows about the long-term effect?

Saved from the Congo Carnage

Hulda Brown in the Congo, 1964

Events in our remote location in the jungle of northeast Congo had begun to puzzle us. We had been told that rebel troops had moved into the area and had released all of the prisoners from the local jail. There were also rumours of young men being trained in the jungle. About four years previously, the Congo had been granted its independence from Belgium, and after several years of civil unrest, things had finally settled down. Or had they? Something was brewing and we didn't know what it was. We had no television or telephone. Radio news was very limited in our remote area, and all mail services had stopped. We knew my family in Canada, and Aubrey's family in Australia, would be concerned about us.

At one point, I decided not to follow my feelings and simply read my scheduled morning scripture passage in Luke 2. I felt comfort in the words of twelve-year-old Jesus, *"Know ye not that I must be about My Father's business?"* I rested in that.

So, despite the unrest in the country, we carried on as best we could with classes for prospective Bible school students and with our regular church services. Our three oldest children had fortunately just returned home from boarding school and they, together with our six-year-old, needed to be entertained. Aubrey started the twins on French lessons for an hour each day. Ronnie, two years older than Kenny and Carol, helped me with food preparations, and this help was to prove invaluable in the weeks ahead.

On November 4th, 1964, while I was still in my morning meeting with the school children, two rebel soldiers—Simbas as they liked to be known—came onto our mission station. When I arrived back at our house, I found them there, intent on searching the house. After carefully going through every room and drawer in our home looking for radio transmitters and weapons, and finding nothing, they ordered Aubrey to go with them to prison. Calmly, he picked up his Bible and a blanket, said good-bye to us, and followed them on the two-kilometre walk to our little town of Poko. I stood on the steps of our home with the four children, and we watched him disappear down the hill with the armed guards.

Trouble had gone from rumour to reality. When Aubrey arrived at the prison, he found thirteen other white men already there: a Belgian priest, and several Greek and Belgian plantation owners. Thus, began days of added suspense: not knowing what was going on, but being fully aware that we were in a precarious situation.

That night I tucked each of the children into their beds and under their mosquito nets. The netting would keep them safe from the mosquitoes, but what would keep them safe from these Simbas? I did the only thing I could do: I committed them into the care of our all-wise and all-powerful God. Then I took my Bible and drew up a chair beside my own bed. I put my storm lantern on the chair, crawled into bed under my own mosquito net, and then opened my Bible to 2 Chronicles 20. This was a passage that a fellow missionary had given to us in a previous letter.

"O our God, wilt thou not judge them? For we have no might against this great company that comes against us: neither know we what to do: but our eyes are upon you.... For the battle is not yours, but God's...ye shall not need to fight in this battle: set yourselves, stand ye still, and see the salvation of the Lord...the Lord will be with you." Again, it was God's word that stilled my heart and mind.

I thanked God, blew out my lantern, closed my eyes, and had a good sleep. The next day dawned bleak. Our husband and father was in prison. We knew that the Simbas would not feed him, so we asked them, through a messenger, if we could send food to the prisoners. The rebels agreed. So, we went to work, Ronnie and I, each making a batch of bread. We killed our last rabbit, and cooked it up in a nice meal which we sent down to the men. The children and I licked the pots. With each meal, the children sent notes to their dad, hidden in the food, and when the empty pots and pans returned there would be a little message for us hidden somewhere.

Aubrey had gone to prison on Wednesday. On Friday, I asked the pastor and some of the elders to come to our house to pray. When they came, we read Acts 12, of Peter's release from prison. That gave us stimulus for prayer. The next day was Saturday and our pastor went down to the rebel captain and asked if Mr. Brown could come home for church the next day. The pastor told him that we needed Mr. Brown to preach and lead the service. The captain scratched his head for a bit and then said, "Okay, Mr. Brown can go back for the church meeting with a guard, but he must come right back after the service."

Sunday morning finally came and the children waited eagerly for the first sign of their daddy coming up the road. When they saw him coming with his guard, they raced to meet him. The guard followed us all into the church, put his spear up against the wall, and then, (hopefully) listened. My husband performed his duties in the church service, and all too soon the meeting was over. I was hoping that he would be able to come and have a cup of tea with me before he went back, but that was not in the guard's plans. Aubrey was marched right back to the prison.

The next day, Monday, at about five o'clock in the afternoon and without any notice, a truck drove up to our house. Out stepped Aubrey. When he asked them what he was supposed to do now, they replied, "Just stay in your house. You are under house arrest!" God had answered our prayers.

Aubrey had been in prison for six days and it was good to have him back home. Although we were all back together again, we were conscious of the fact that our situation was still a perilous one. There were rumours of the rebels fighting with government troops, and foreign forces were beginning to get involved. Anti-American sentiment was beginning to build again and that usually meant anyone with white skin was a target. Did anyone know we were in danger?

I remember how often, after the children were asleep, I went upstairs to their bedroom attic window, and looked out into the night, searching for some sign of a plane. Was anyone thinking of us? Was anyone coming to get us? But there was no response from that beautiful night sky and the twinkling stars. Aubrey's thoughts about a rescue must have been similar to mine—though somewhat more practical, for one day I saw him cutting down a very nice tree we had in the middle of our compound. He was making room for a helicopter to land.

During the daytime, we were always tense not knowing when and where the Simbas would come around. Often, they just seemed to appear.

I remember one day several of them came and settled in the shade of a tree in our backyard. I had clothes on the line and needed to bring them in, but I was afraid to go out there. We had been told that the Simbas thought our fear proved we were guilty of wrongdoing. So finally, I picked up all the courage I could muster, braced myself, and went to get my clothes off the line. They watched me, but said and did nothing. Even as I had watched for planes at night, they too, were watching for planes in the sky. Their thinking was that if rescuers would come for us, they would quickly kill us first.

The weeks dragged by and the tension grew. I would manage until about 11 a.m. then I would say to my husband, "Let's go and pray." I felt I couldn't take anymore. We would go to the bedroom and pray, which then gave us fresh courage to keep on going in those monotonous days filled with tension and uneasiness.

I remember one particular evening, darkness had settled, and we had closed our doors for the night. Suddenly, there was a loud banging on the door. We were afraid and did not open it right away. After threats of breaking the door down, we reluctantly opened the doors to some obviously drugged and drunk Simbas, brandishing spears and machetes—their killing gear. In a frantic effort to calm and stall them, we invited them in and offered them chairs and some coffee and bread. They quietly ate and drank our offerings, and then mysteriously left without a word. We closed and locked the doors almost collapsing with relief. We had heard of many other similar situations where the rebels had come at night, slit the throat of their victims and then left. We could find no other reason for their visit, but something had stopped them from fulfilling their intentions. God's power was evident that night.

Psalm 27:2 says, *"when evil men advance against me to devour my flesh, when my enemies and my foes attack me, they will stumble and fall."*

We were thankful and often amazed that the children always seemed to be able to go to sleep when they went to bed. My husband and I went to bed that night, too, but not to sleep. We were too frightened. We shivered with fear and cold. We took turns praying, first one, then the other; back and forth we went until 3:30 in the morning. Somehow, by then we felt a certain peace, and fitfully slept for a few hours.

Word reached us that Belgian paratroopers had dropped from American planes into Paulis (our nearest major town) to rescue hostages. They had just completed a successful drop on Stanleyville, a large city four hundred kilometres southwest of us where there were several hundred hostages. As the soldiers dropped from the sky into Paulis, the Simbas killed nineteen Europeans, including Mr. Jay Tucker, an American missionary. Our children wept when they heard this news, as he was the father of two of their school friends.

Things were reaching a critical point. Did anybody know we were here on our little station at Poko? The day following a night of prayer, a big truck drove up onto our compound and parked. This seemed very odd, but we had heard that rebels were running off with hostages, and wondered if the truck was there for that same reason. We were very conscious that we were in extreme danger, but knew that prayer could change things. We asked the Lord to remove the truck from our compound.

The next day was Sunday. In the morning, the truck started up and drove off. Shortly, we heard from our Africans on the station that many of the Simbas from Poko had fled during the night. That was a relief, but what did it mean.

It was the 29th of November. We started yet another quiet day in our house as we had been told to do by the Simbas. The Africans had the Sunday morning service as per usual, and in the evening, we asked many of the people from the church to come and join us on our veranda for some fellowship. We had a lovely time talking, singing and praying together. We did not know that night, that it would be the last time we would meet with these dear friends.

November 30 is a day our family will never forget. The morning dawned quiet and sullen. Our Simba guard came along as usual near midday, carrying his gun and spear. He sat down on our veranda to chat, and was soon into his favourite rant—denouncing white people. "They put minced-up black people into cans and sell it as corned beef," he would say. At noon he got up and said, "I'll be back at four."

An hour later, we had just finished our lunch. Dominique, one of our friends, came running up to our house, and yelled out to our son Ron, "I have just heard shooting in the town!" Ron ran inside to tell us. We quickly locked our doors and closed the shutters that covered our glassless windows. Then all six of us lined up and peeked through the cracks. We did not know what to expect, but we prayed that it was our rescuers—whoever they may be. Each minute seemed like an eternity.

Soon we heard the sound of vehicles climbing up the hill to our house. We could hear them long before we could see them. Shooting as they came, soldiers in a jeep and a large army truck raced up to our front door and the leader jumped out with his gun at the ready and shouted, "Come out, you're safe!" What welcome words—they spoke English, and they were friends. We threw open the doors and with all our hugs, laughter, and tears, I think they felt it had been worth their while finding this family at Poko.

The soldiers were from 52 Commando, a ground unit of mostly Rhodesian and South African mercenaries who had been hired by the Congolese government. Their job was to clear out all the remaining hostages scattered on plantations and mission stations throughout the vast jungle area of northeast Congo. Three of this unit had been shot along the way as they risked their lives in this communist-inspired uprising that had little to do with them. We were so thankful for them and we soon realised that once again, God had intervened.

As a dutiful hostess I quickly made some tea and served it to them, then rushed around, picking up a few things to take with us—wherever we were going. The soldiers had given us just a few minutes. We already had several suitcases packed in readiness, but I felt there should be some last-minute things to pick up. My mind being in a whirl with all the excitement, I picked up an alarm clock and some little knives out of my cutlery drawer. Next, I went into the bedroom, opened our locked trunk and pulled out a heavy blanket for the journey. That latter item was a good choice, but the former items had no rhyme or reason. I left my pretty china teacups on the coffee table in the living room, along with all our other possessions. These suddenly had very little meaning.

The soldiers loaded our few bags into the truck and we were taken to the central business area of Poko where we would wait for the convoy to assemble. Upon our arrival there, we were told of the Simbas' plan to take us all to Paulis at four o'clock to be executed. This is why our Simba guard had told us he'd be back at that time. God was on time and even two hours early.

We waited in one of the government offices near where Aubrey had been in prison; excited at being rescued, but realising we were still not out of danger. A small contingent of soldiers stayed to guard the town centre while the others were out collecting all the other expatriates from the various plantations and the Catholic mission station.

While we waited the children were quiet and cooperative, but the strain of the fear and excitement was beginning to show. The soldiers started shooting again, much of it up into the air to remind the rebels of their superior weapons. Many of the bullets were falling back onto the corrugated tin roof and making an awful sound. Only once did I hear one of the children complain. While we were huddled under a sturdy wooden table, little six-year-old David blurted out, "Oh, I wish we could get out of here!"

Within a few hours, the convoy had assembled and we were ready to move down the road towards safety and out of rebel territory. The mercenaries recaptured our Chevrolet Carryall that the Simbas had confiscated. We had only owned it for four months and Aubrey asked if the mercenaries would drive it out for us.

They agreed, but when the convoy started up the vehicle wasn't running properly and rather than risk the rebels fixing it and chasing the convoy, our rescuers thought it best to disable it. That was done efficiently by a single grenade. We had just rounded a corner and were thus spared the pain of seeing this almost-new vehicle go up in smoke and flames. Our fifteen and thirteen-year-old boys were very saddened by this but, when your life is at stake, nothing else matters.

Three rough and frightful hours passed as we made our way to a town called Dingela, where there was a large Catholic mission station with an airstrip. Here we would wait for a plane to take us to the capital city, Leopoldville. After about an hour of travel in the convoy, we suddenly noticed a truck following us. It was full of Simbas. We pounded on the cab of our truck and the truck stopped abruptly. One of the jeeps swung around immediately and the mercenaries fired their big machine gun at the Simba truck. It skidded to a stop and the rebels fled into the forest.

During the rest of the trip, we only encountered a few rebel roadblocks, whose spear-carrying guards proved no match for machine guns. Upon our arrival at Dingela, we were offered food and a bed. What a horrendous day it had been, and the safe bed was a welcome treat.

We stayed there three days, waiting for a plane. In the common area there was a radio transmitter and receiver to keep in contact with the planes. One day we heard this on the radio: "Does anybody know the whereabouts of the Aubrey Brown family?" That was music to our ears. Somebody was concerned and looking for us. The next day, December 3, the first DC-3 plane arrived to pick up refugees. Because of the children we were allowed on this first one. We did not know until we arrived in Leopoldville, that two of our fellow-missionaries had been killed in Stanleyville along with about fifty other hostages. Later on, we heard of another two of our friends and fellow-workers killed at Wamba.

Our deliverance was nothing less than a miracle and the many people that prayed for us during this time were definitely part of this miracle. How we praised God for our African friends who had stayed with us until our rescue. These included the two men who were our domestic helpers, as well as the pastor and our students. Most of the other village people had fled to the forest for safety. That ended our ninety-eight days of terror. God does hear and answer prayer.

My brother Henry, a pastor in Morden, Manitoba, had his congregation fast and pray for our safety. He told us that the morning after their day of prayer they had heard on the radio of our safety! What a thrill that was to his congregation.

There are, indeed, many more miracles that could be cited, but I will mention just one more, which is rather unique. There was an African church elder who was witnessing for the Lord during this time of rebellion. The Simbas tried to kill him, but he escaped for a time. He finally had to flee into the grassland, where tall, dry stands of elephant grass can easily hide anything within it. The rebels followed him, surrounded his hideout, and set fire to the grass, thinking he'd perish. The fire was all around the man, and as it drew nearer and nearer, he became desperate.

He prayed, "Lord, you are the God of Shadrach, Meshach and Abednego. What you did for them, you can do for me." As the fire got nearer to him, it gradually died down and went out. He was spared! God is still in the business of miracles today. Hallelujah! This man lived to prove that. God did indeed become more real to us through these experiences. Nevertheless, God's plan was not to save all his servants from death. Several of our fellow missionaries became martyrs in what some have called the Congo Carnage.

Story extracted from the book, ***River of Memories*** *(2001) by Hulda Brown*.

Overcoming Obstacles or Uphill Home

Linda Nagel in Côte d'Ivoire, 1986

"It's been a long time since you've been to my village," said the man from the small village of Koning.

"Have they done any work on the road?" I asked, knowing how inaccessible the village was at times.

"It's in really good shape now," he replied. "The grader has just gone over it so the cotton trucks can get in."

"In that case we'll come tomorrow," I quickly replied, recalling our prayer for guidance as to which villages to visit that week.

Friday morning, we all piled into the car, taking along pictures, Bibles and an accordion—our tools for evangelism, as well as a good supply of water. Helen brought along cookies for a snack, although not for herself. She rarely indulged in sweets but loved to bake.

Few villages were situated on main roads. We prepared for a challenge every time we went out to these remote places. I drove slowly by faith, hoping the fragile bridges would hold. Driving uphill toward the village wasn't a problem but when we started down the steep grade on the other side, we soon realised it wouldn't be easy. I felt my body tensing as I pumped the brakes while weaving around or going over big rocks jutting up from the trail. If a grader had gone over this, its blade had surely been in the air all the way down. Perhaps the man who gave the report had been over the road only on his bicycle.

"We can get down alright, but getting back out of this village might be a different story," I commented with little faith. With no place to turn around or back up our only choice was to keep moving in the direction we were going, straight down. A crowd gathered to welcome us as we drove into the village at the bottom of the hill. Visits from foreigners were rare. We shook hands with everyone while being led to the shade of a big mango tree. They gathered chairs for us to sit, and the chief called the people together to hear what we had to say. Both Helen and Alfred shared stories of Jesus and the people listened well. Afterwards they took us to see some villagers who were ill. I gave basic medicine and we prayed for them. A couple of hours passed before we left the village, and the whole time—I'm ashamed to say—my thoughts were on the hill. How were we going to get out of there?

Finally, we went on our way, with the yams, rice and a live chicken they insisted on giving us. At the bottom of the menacing hill, we stopped to pray. "Lord help us get up this hill without breaking something in the car. We're a long way from home (as if he didn't know!)" Pauline, Alfred's wife, was pregnant with their third child, and the thought of walking many kilometres in the hot sun wasn't too appealing to her.

Helen and Alfred opted to walk up the hill to lighten the load. With my foot hard on the gas pedal, I charged forward, up and over the first big rock, swerving around a pointed stone, over another rock and another. Bump, bump, up, up and up. I could hear Pauline praying in the back seat as I tried to keep us moving forward. If the car stalled, we wouldn't make the steep grade.

Whew! We made it to the top of that treacherous hill. All we could say was, "Thank you Jesus, thank you Jesus." I knew God had his hand on the steering wheel. We had a praise meeting before continuing our journey home.

Beyond the Mud *(2015) by Linda Nagel, page 128.*

Victory at the Bridge

Walter Mohr in Indonesia, 1978

It was rainy season but had not rained for several days. We had unwisely driven our Volkswagen van about seven kilometres on a narrow mud road to the small village church in Java. A local believer waiting at the highway had urged us to drive in rather than walk. I hesitated but followed his advice. We were here for a farewell meal and service—soon our family would fly back to Canada. We enjoyed the feast of food and fine fellowship. I had just begun to preach when heavy raindrops began pounding on the roof. I hastened to conclude my message and holding plastic sheets over our heads we scurried to the van. We were experiencing a heavy torrential rainy season downpour. A few of the young men jumped into the van in case we needed help.

Indeed, we soon needed help badly. We had driven about two kilometres when we came to the steep slope leading downward to the small bridge crossing the swollen creek. Going down was easy although the van was slithering and sliding but we saw that part of the log-bridge had been washed out. We stopped. Several young men jumped out, pushed the dislodged logs back into place and the bridge was repaired. Crossing the little bridge was easy but climbing the hill beyond was impossible. We tried to move upward with a full van hoping the weight would give us the traction needed. That failed. Then everyone jumped out in the rain to push the van but the mud was deep and the wheels simply spun. We prayed and tried again and again—

backward and forward, backward and forward, but we were truly stuck. We were also soaking wet and splattered with mud.

In frustration and hopelessness, we gave up trying. Most of the young men ran back to the village. The news they were carrying was not good. The two leading church elders were deeply troubled. Meanwhile we decided that Melita and the three younger children should walk up the hill through the mud toward the highway about five kilometres away. They would look for a taxi that could take them to the hotel we had left a few hours prior. Philip and I would stay in the village until we could get the van unstuck and back on the highway. We were on the only road leading in and out.

As Philip and I trudged back toward the village my mind was in turmoil. We had arranged a full schedule. This was the first of nine villages we were to visit. There were no phones to explain our predicament to those churches. "Why had I been so foolish? Did I not realize that this was the rainy season and it might rain any moment, perhaps even every day for the next few months? When would this road be dry enough to get the van out?" We discussed the poverty and isolation of this village. Where would we stay? What would we eat? Where would we sleep? The prospect looked gloomy and darkness was falling. I was wondering too—how would Melita and the three younger children get to the hotel where we had come from that day? Would they find a taxi? Thankfully the rain had slowed to a drizzle.

We had walked about a kilometre when we were met by two church elders. Each one had a small rope in his hand. "Where are you going?" I asked. "To help pull the van out," was their simple reply. I knew it was impolite to laugh but questioned how small ropes could be of any help in getting the van up the hill. Then one elder spoke up. "You are probably not aware of this, but evil spirits control that bridge. If the van cannot move from the bridge and get up that slope the people in this area will know that Satan is stronger than God. We have to pray." Humanly speaking things looked bleak but we walked back with a new urgency. However, I had absolutely no faith that these little ropes plus two older men would get us up the steep muddy hill.

When we reached the van one elder asked where he should tie the rope. I replied that it did not matter but perhaps the front bumper was a good spot.

They hastened to put the rope in place. Then the two elders asked that I join them in prayer at the front of the van. I will never forget Pak Surat's simple Javanese prayer. "Father in heaven, in the name of Jesus Christ we bind the evil spirits and the powers of darkness and set this van free. Amen." Then he said, "Start up the van and drive." And I did.

Yes, we did have two older men slipping and sliding in the mud along with a few young men all pulling the rope. We also had several young men, including our son Philip, pushing the van. But something unbelievable was happening. Miraculously the van moved steadily upward to the top of the hill. For me, and for all who were present, it was truly an unforgettable experience. It felt surreal, as though angels were pushing us up the slope. Minutes later we were on level ground shaking hands and saying goodbye to these precious brothers.

Not much later Melita and the three younger children were amazed to see lights coming toward them. They had walked almost four kilometres praying for a miracle and wondering when we would all be united again as a family. You can be sure we had a praise party.

Interestingly eight years later Melita and I were back in Indonesia riding in a taxi to visit that village church again. It was the dry season and mud was not a concern. There were no cows on the road and no one was walking nearby yet strangely when we got to the small bridge the taxi driver honked his horn. I asked him why he did this. "I always salute the spirits," he replied. Praise God for men of faith who did not believe in saluting the spirits but in binding and disarming them!

A Gem Sparkles in the Desert

Wilfred Watson in Venezuela, 1961

When Wilfred ventured into a mountainous desert in Venezuela, he found two abandoned evangelical churches. He contacted their mother church and they encouraged him to reopen the buildings.

For several months, every Sunday with a small accordion and a bicycle in the back of his pickup truck, Wilfred drove 64 kilometres on a dangerous, sandy, twisty Pan American Highway, crossed a dry riverbed, then continued on through the desert to one of these churches.

Then one week, water washing down from the mountains filled the riverbed. Could he drive through? Wilfred waded into the river up to his belt and knew the truck wouldn't make it. He then strapped his accordion to his back, lifted up his bicycle and carried it across—on the downside of the flow so that if he tripped over a stone, he wouldn't become entangled and possibly drown.

On the other side of the river, he pedaled six kilometres through loose sand. He pushed the bike forward sweating and praying, "Lord, you know I like to see things happen. I've been coming to El Habra for several months and nothing has happened. Lord, I ask you to do something today. Indicate whether I should be coming here or not. If I don't get a sign, this is the last time I'm coming."

He opened the church and dusted the crude benches. The few regulars sauntered in, deadpan expressions on their faces without even a good morning for the preacher—most uninspiring. With the accordion Wilf led the singing, then he prayed, read scripture, and took the offering. He was about to preach the sermon when in walked a young woman with long black hair and with two shy little girls hiding behind her skirt. At the door she removed her walking slippers and donned a pair of shiny shoes. She marched up to the second row along with her girls. As Wilf preached, she nodded her head in agreement. "Is there anyone here who would like to be saved, to let the Lord Jesus come into your life and give you hope of eternal life?" he asked.

The eager young mother raised her hand, stood and said, "I have come to be saved."

After the closing hymn Wilf invited one of the men to stay while he reexplained the gospel to Hilda. She couldn't read, but he opened the Bible to John 3:16 and other verses. He led her in prayer asking the Lord to forgive her sins, to come into her heart and save her. As they walked to the back of the church and he was locking up, Hilda said, "Would you come to my home?"

"Where do you live Hilda?" he asked.

"Guaidi, about six kilometres up the river bottom."

Wilf considered the trip there and back by bike, wading across the river to his truck and then driving the 64 kilometres home to his wife Elizabeth and the children.

"Sister Hilda, if I can ford the river with my truck two weeks from today, I'll go and preach at your home."

Two weeks later the water had receded. Hilda was at the church when he arrived. After the service Hilda asked again, "Brother Wilfredo, are you coming to my home as you promised?"

"Yes ma'am."

One of the men accompanied them sitting in the back of the truck with the bike and accordion. Up the river bottom, and around huge stones they pressed on. Wilf pictured Hilda with her little girls walking that long hot distance to find salvation. At last, they came to her home, high on a bank overlooking the dry riverbed. Under a big tree in the yard Hilda had arranged log seating for 40 people.

"Lord, she must have faith," Wilf mused.

What a sight. People dressed in their very best emerged from the mountains, joyously greeting Wilfred and introducing themselves.

Hilda helped Wilf with the singing as he led and played his accordion. He introduced a few choruses, read the Bible, and prayed. Hilda approached him and whispered. "Brother Wilfredo don't forget to give an invitation. Seven people are going to be saved."

Following the sermon Wilf gave the invitation and seven people responded. Hilda had been preparing these people to come forward.

Promising to return in two weeks, Wilf hurried home to share the thrill with Elizabeth.

On the next visit to El Habra, Hilda was there once again with her children. After the typical service, with just one live parishioner in the otherwise dead church, Wilf eagerly loaded the truck and off they bounced to Guaidi. Again, the people came and again Hilda whispered in Wilf's ear. "Brother Wilfredo, be sure to give an invitation. Five more are going to be saved."

Sure enough, when the invitation was given five prepared souls responded and were led into the Kingdom of God.

"It wasn't the result of a sermon preached," Wilf later told Elizabeth, "but Hilda's humble efforts prior to the service."

Hilda taught herself to read by memorising verses in the Bible and studying each word. Whether she learned to read anything else or not, she learned to read the Bible. At the dedication of their small church building, she read a full psalm perfectly. Wilf almost cried looking at her—

God's chosen vessel.

Thirty years later, Hilda, her husband, and their five children are walking with the Lord. Their second daughter has graduated from Bible school and she and her sister are both wives of pastors.

Attitude of Gratitude *(1992) by Virginia Tait, pages 67-70.*

XIV

Short God Stories

Bring joy to your servant, Lord, for I put my trust in you.
Psalm 86:4

As you will have noticed, Leaves to the Nations is full of God stories. He is still working today as he did in Bible times. We serve an awesome God.
These next few stories are delightful snippets of the WEC missionary experience. We include them here to put a smile on your face and to further inspire your trust in the Lord.

Short God Stories

A Bowl of Reese Puffs

Fred in Asia, 2023

When I arrived in the capital last week I walked by a market and was surprised to see my favourite cereal, Reese Puffs, which is very rarely available here. I asked the cashier how much it was and he said, "Twenty dollars,"—crazy expensive. As I was returning the box to the shelf the owner said, "Let's go into the back and have a bowl together and it's on me."

I said "no," but he insisted so we sat down and had a nice bowl of Reese Puffs together. He gave me the rest of the cereal along with the milk as a gift. And yes, we got to talk about Jesus. The owner of the store, who is from an unreached area of the country, heard the good news that day.

* * *

A Memorable Prayer Meeting

WEC Headquarters in Toronto, 1940's

There was a great need for male missionaries in a little place called "Mitu" (pronounced Me Too), in South America. One of our single-girl candidates took up the prayer request and started fervently praying, "Men for me too!" Needless to say, it was hilarious and we all started laughing hard, forcing our meeting to an early close.

* * *

A Toggle Switch

Suzanne Adamson in the UK, 2020's

At Betel Jan, a recovering alcoholic, and I spent many of our days out delivering flyers. Jan's daughter had gotten her an MP3 player so she could listen to music while she walked. But no matter what Jan did, she couldn't hear the music. I asked her if I could help so I had a fiddle and still nothing. She decided to give up and put the device away. In so doing, she exclaimed, "me toggles in me ear." She had been using the end of the string for her hood as an earphone.

* * *

Catching Garbage

Maria Swan (age 12) in Chad 2020's

There is lots of garbage in the city. When the wind comes up just before rainy season and it is kind of stormy, the wind makes the garbage fly in the air and my friends and I try to catch it. That is one of our favourite games.

* * *

Fitness Class?

Danae in Central Asia, 2023

Office conversation: "But if my wife exercises, she will be easier to steal!" is an argument that one of our male staff has against me starting up a fitness class. I guess if your wife is difficult to carry, she is more likely to remain with you. I thoroughly enjoy these glimpses into the minds of the people around me.

* * *

Seed Brings Fruit in God's Time

Amy in the Middle East, 2024

I have been hearing stories from around the country of seeds that have been sown a long time ago and are finally ready to be harvested. Stories of people who have had New Testaments just sitting on shelves for years finally noticing and reading them, or people wondering about Christianity for a long time but are now seeking out a church to learn more. It feels like we are in a new season.

* * *

Three Soldiers Came in my Bedroom

Ethan Swan (age 7) in Chad 2023

I was in my bed one morning, very early, and I heard some yelling or something. Then three soldiers came in the bedroom. I wasn't really surprised to see them because I knew there had been shooting in town and sometimes, they came around to our house. They had come before. I didn't get up out of bed though because I didn't want to get in their way. I figured they were looking for guns or checking to see if we were robbers or something. They didn't find any guns even though we did have some—toy guns in the birthday box.

* * *

Trusting Neighbours in 1998

Caroline Brown in Türkiye

We hadn't been in Türkiye for many months but were about to be travelling for a few days. I needed someone to look after our pet budgie. I just happened to see my upstairs neighbour on the street, and she stopped to greet me. I asked (or at least tried to ask) if she could look after our budgie while we were away. She seemed surprised and asked me several times to repeat my request and then asked a few questions. When she seemed to understand she said yes.

Later I brought the bird cage containing the budgie to her door. She looked at me blankly, I tried to explain again that I wanted her to look after my bird. She burst out laughing and explained that she thought I was asking her, an almost stranger, to look after my four-year-old daughter. No wonder she looked surprised. How amazing that she would agree.

* * *

Trusting Neighbours in 2009

Caroline Brown in the Middle East

My neighbour across the hallway had recently become the caregiver to her baby grandson after her son and daughter-in-law had separated. She came to my door with the baby in her arms and a bottle of formula, and asked if I could look after the baby. She said she was just going to be gone for an hour and the baby should sleep all the time once he'd drank his milk, and then she was gone. It was all so sudden and unexpected, I was taken off guard, I wasn't even the sort that wanted to hold other people's babies and didn't consider myself good with them. My neighbour—who barely knew me—trusted me with this precious child. This was an honour yet daunting.

The baby didn't sleep long, and the hour stretched into three or more, while I cuddled and rocked the restless child without even a clean diaper for him. Needless to say, I was relieved when she came back, and I could return the baby.

Manufactured by Amazon.ca
Bolton, ON

45475207R00166